MARC

Tips

SOUTH AFRICA

www.marco-polo.com

← INSIDE FRONT COVER: THE BEST HIGHLIGHTS

The best Insider Tips → p. 4

Best of ... → p. 6

Cape Provinces → p. 32

Cape Town & surrounds → p. 48

SYMBOLS

INSIDER TIP	Insider Tip
★	Highlight
●●●●	Best of ...
(scenic view symbol)	Scenic view

Responsible travel: for ecological or fair trade aspects

PRICE CATEGORIES HOTELS

Expensive	over 1200 rand
Moderate	750–1200 rand
Budget	under 750 rand

Price for a double room with breakfast per night

PRICE CATEGORIES RESTAURANTS

Expensive	over 200 rand
Moderate	150–200 rand
Budget	under 150 rand

Prices based on an average meal including starter, main course and dessert

On the cover: The Golden Gate Highlands National Park p. 70 | Golf in the Wild p. 102

CONTENTS

Free State → p. 66

KwaZulu-Natal → p. 72

Northern Provinces → p. 80

Road atlas → p. 120

DID YOU KNOW?

Timeline → p. 12
Post World Cup South Africa → p. 21
Local specialities → p. 26
Diamond diving → p. 47
Books & films → p. 91
Currency converter → p. 114
Budgeting → p. 115
Weather in Johannesburg → p. 116

MAPS IN THE GUIDEBOOK
(122 A1) Page numbers and coordinates refer to the road atlas
(0) Site/address located off the map. Coordinates are also given for places that are not marked on the road atlas
(U A1) Refers to the street map of Cape town inside the back cover
Street map of Johannesburg → p. 130/131

INSIDE BACK COVER: PULL-OUT MAP →

PULL-OUT MAP 🗺
(🗺 A–B 2–3) Refers to the removable pull-out map
(🗺 a–b 2–3) Refers to the additional insert map on the pull-out map

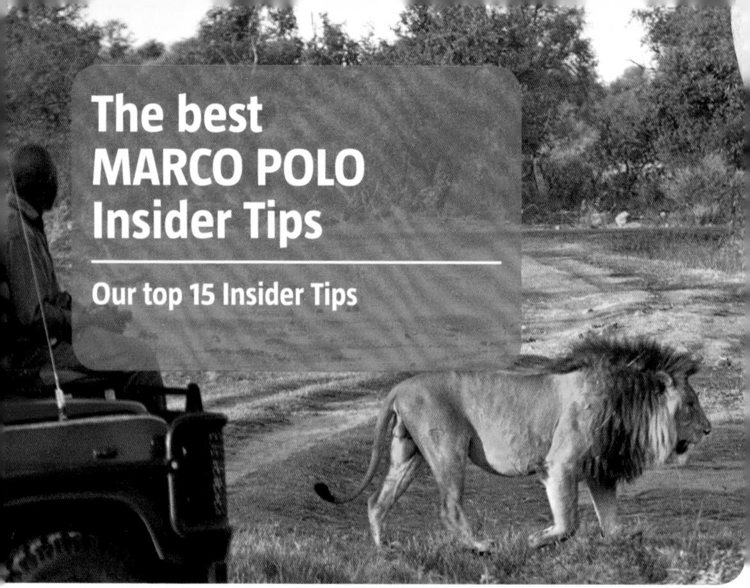

The best MARCO POLO Insider Tips

Our top 15 Insider Tips

INSIDER TIP The name says it all
Located high above Wilderness' 5km (3mi) stretch of pristine beach is the boutique hotel *Views*. The hotel's glass exterior and its blue, white and beige interiors mean that it blends perfectly into its beach front setting → p. 36

INSIDER TIP Out of Africa
Get kitted out for your African safari at Port Elizabeth's *Melville & Moon* – one of South Africa's best suppliers for the great outdoors → p. 46

INSIDER TIP Half-price sundowners
Take advantage of the Table Mountain special – cable car rides are a half price bargain at sunset in the summer months (photo right) → p. 53

INSIDER TIP Born to be wild
Let your hair down and hire the latest in bikes from *Harley Davidson* in Cape Town and book your biker tour for anywhere in the country → p. 103

INSIDER TIP Sea view
Get some of the best Indian Ocean views at the small *Beach House* B & B in the world famous surfers' paradise of Jeffrey's Bay. Make sure that you ask for the corner guest bedroom on the first floor → p. 47

INSIDER TIP Simply delicious
One of Cape Town's top chefs, Franck Dangereux, owns and runs the country-style *Foodbarn Restaurant* in the leafy and quiet suburb of Noordhoek where he serves up unpretentious but top class cuisine → p. 53

INSIDER TIP In vino veritas
Doolhof wine estate near Paarl produces excellent wines and visitors can also stay over in the manor house → p. 63

INSIDER TIP Candle craze
The *Kapula Gallery* in Bredasdorp sells colourful candles with African designs→ p. 58

INSIDER TIP Party in Jozi

With its glass décor, *Randlords* – a glitzy nightclub located on the 22nd floor of an office block in downtown Johannesburg – has fast become the latest hotspot for the city's trendy in-crowd → p. 86

INSIDER TIP Gourmet getaway

Take time out and treat yourself to some peace and tranquility with a stay at the *Cleopatra Mountain Farmhouse* in the majestic Drakensberg. There are crystal clear river streams, waterfalls, mountains and memorable five-star fare served every evening → p. 79

INSIDER TIP Pedal power

Steep descents down Table Mountain: only for daredevil mountain bikers → p. 100

INSIDER TIP A hotel true to its name

Downtown Johannesburg is undergoing a revival: try the ultra-modern and very affordable *Lamunu* which means 'orange' in seSotho → p. 86

INSIDER TIP Tee off in the wild

For a rather unique sporting experience try the *Hans Merensky Golf Course* where elephants and giraffes make up the spectators → p. 102

INSIDER TIP Malaria-free in the bush

There are a number of draw cards for the expansive state-run *Madikwe Game Reserve* in the North West Province (bordering on Botswana). It is in a region with an incredible diversity of species, it is malaria-free and it is never crowded as day visitors are not permitted and the number of guests it plays host to at any given time is limited to 300 (photo left) → p. 93

INSIDER TIP A powerhouse stay

The old power station on Knysna lagoon has recently been converted into the *Turbine Hotel*. The boutique hotel is an eclectic mix of industrial design and art – its old industrial machinery is under heritage protection → p. 42

BEST OF ...

GREAT PLACES FOR FREE

Discover new places and save money

FOR FREE

● ***Glistening diamonds***

Documenting the exciting era of the diamond rush is the *Big Hole and Kimberley Mine Museum*. Whereas there is an admission charge for the former, entrance to the museum is free. Several thousand genuine diamonds can be viewed in the *diamond vault* → p. 38

● ***Giants of the deep***

The small coastal town of *Hermanus* is renowned as a whale watching venue. Every year between June and December hundreds of whales from the Antarctic converge in the bay and can be viewed from the shore — a very special sight — and it's free (photo) → p. 61

● ***Climb up Table Mountain***

Its fascinating flora and breathtaking views make the free three-hour hike up the front of Table Mountain unique – start several hundred metres past the cable car base station on the demarcated *Platteklip Gorge* hiking trail → p. 53

● ***Priceless***

The *Tatham Art Gallery* in Pietermaritzburg displays some excellent contemporary South African and international art. Admission is free of charge and on Wednesdays there is the added bonus of a concert → p. 78

● ***Bloemfontein on foot***

Not only does a hike through the *Franklin Game Reserve* introduce you to the flora of the region, but it will also take you past giraffes, buck and other wild animals – all for free → p. 102

● ***Flora and fauna for free***

The *Garden Route* is famous for its abundance of indigenous fauna and flora and there are lots of signboards with informative facts. Conservation and research are a priority so there is no charge → p. 32

●●●● Dots in guidebook refer to 'Best of ...' tips

ONLY IN SOUTH AFRICA
Unique experiences

● *Golf – the people's sport*

In South Africa golf is not a luxury sport. As space is not an issue even the smallest towns have at least a nine-hole golf course. Wear whatever takes your fancy – only the big city clubs have a dress code. You will find the highest density of golf courses in George on the Garden Route where the *Fancourt Estate Club* lies in an area of outstanding natural beauty → p. 35

● *The perfect wave*

Surfers rate the small town of *Jeffrey's Bay* near Port Elizabeth as the best surf spot on the African continent. Here they can catch the perfect wave at the Super Tubes break (photo) → p. 47

● *Nothing paltry about this poultry*

South Africans are known for their love of meat, especially big steaks prepared on a *braai*. For the more health conscious, ostrich meat is becoming increasingly popular – the meat is tasty but low in fat and cholesterol. Visit the *Cango Ostrich Farm* in Oudtshoorn to learn more → p. 36

● *A sunset to remember*

Sundowners are an institution in South Africa so what better place to enjoy yours than on top of the *Franschhoek Pass.* With views across the valley almost as far as Cape Town and a bottle of your favourite regional wine in hand – life is beautiful → p. 59

● *A journey through time*

The *Basotho Cultural Village* in the Free State will give you first-hand insights into how the Basotho have lived for centuries. The mountains that separate South Africa from Lesotho are their home and here visitors get to meet the chief, try the home brew and make the acquaintance of a sangoma → p. 70

● *Under the old oak trees*

Dorp Street in Stellenbosch takes you back in time to how South Africa was in the first decades after the Cape was colonised. The oaks in this street are listed and carry special significance for the town's student population – superstition has it that if an acorn falls on your head you will pass your exams → p. 64

ONLY IN

BEST OF ...

AND IF IT RAINS?

Activities to brighten your day

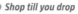

- ***Shop till you drop***
  More people visit the *Victoria & Alfred (V & A for short) Waterfront* in Cape Town than Table Mountain or the pyramids in Egypt. This shopping emporium encompasses several buildings and is part of a working harbour (photo) → p. 53

- ***Long Street Baths***
  Even if the weather is bad in Cape Town you can still go for a swim. Simply head to the historical indoor pool in Long Street → p. 51

- ***Bastion of history***
  The *Castle of Good Hope* is South Africa's oldest building. Today it is home to several museums housing documents and paintings about the history of the Cape → p. 50

- ***A good vintage***
  Wine tasting is always a good way to while away the time when it rains. A good option is the Constantia Wine Route only 20 minutes from central Cape Town with some excellent estates like *Groot Constantia* → p. 51

- ***World Heritage site***
  Located 40km (25mi) from Johannesburg is the *Cradle of Humankind,* a network of sandstone caves in which the fossilised remains of the hominids that roamed Africa several million years ago have been found. The interactive display at the Maropeng Visitor Centre will take you back in time → p. 87

- ***Franschhoek Motor Museum***
  More than 200 cars and motorbikes covering a century of motor vehicle history make this collection on the *L'Ormarins* wine estate one of a kind in South Africa → p. 59

RAIN

RELAX AND CHILL OUT

Take it easy and spoil yourself

CHILL OUT

● ***Mountain escape***

If you want to get away from it all and relax then head to the *Homtini Guest Farm* in the Outeniqua Mountains near Knysna. Pamper body and mind with an aromatherapy massage or enjoy some food for the soul with a relaxing picnic in the wild → **p. 42**

● ***City getaway***

The *One & Only Hotel* is a resort and spa right in middle of Cape Town's V & A Waterfront that offers a varied spa programme with the emphasis on products and plants sourced from Africa. Perfect haven of calm amid the hustle and bustle of the city → **p. 55**

● ***Thai massage in a Cape Dutch setting***

For a special spa experience visit the historic *Vineyard Hotel* in the Cape Town suburb of Newlands. Let the professionally trained Thai therapists revive your body and soul → **p. 56**

● ***On the water's edge***

Water has a very therapeutic role to play in our lives and this fact had a role to play when the architects of *Moyo uShaka* in Durban built a bar at the end of a disused pier, the perfect spot to enjoy that sundowner (photo) → **p. 75**

● ***Traditional healing***

The *Fordoun Hotel & Spa* in KwaZulu-Natal is a resort with a difference. Its owner John collaborated with African traditional healer Dr Elliot Ndlovu to develop treatments and products using indigenous healing plants and age-old local recipes → **p. 78**

● ***Beach restaurant***

Sea, sunshine and a sandy beach – add a cocktail for good measure – and the perfect summer idyll is yours at the *Grand Beach* next to Cape Town's V & A Waterfront. Trendy deckchairs, elegant couches, a beach bar and chic yachts out at sea complete the picture → **p. 53**

INTRODUCTION

DISCOVER SOUTH AFRICA!

South Africa is a massive country and visitors will be spoilt for choice when it comes to things to do. Walks on the Indian Ocean's sandy beaches, hikes along the stunning Garden Route coastline, hot air ballooning, game park excursions, shark-cage diving or whale watching from the coast are but a few of the options on offer. Distances between key cities are huge. Johannesburg is approximately 1600km (1000mi) from Cape Town with the semi-desert Karoo region between the two . The coastline stretches some 3000km (1865mi) along the Atlantic and Indian Oceans.

It is up to you how you choose to explore the country: be it by luxury train, motorbike or by car, which is the best option as the country's main motorways are excellent. Sheep farms that stretch for miles are a common sight and farmers are now also opening their doors to tourists. Hospitality on the farms is first rate and the perfect way to get to know the predominantly Afrikaans rural community. Travel via Kimberley

Photo: A Western Cape beach

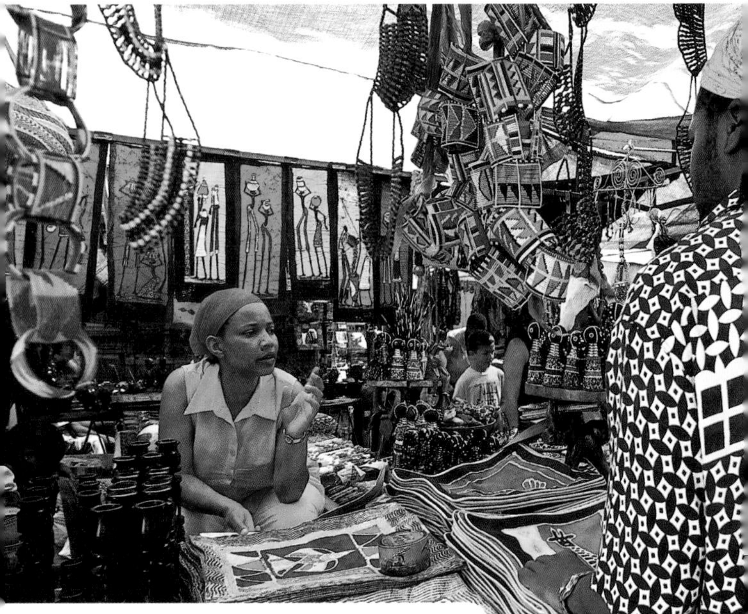

Brightly coloured handcrafts on display in a market in Cape Town

when you do the Johannesburg to Cape Town trip. It is here where the biggest diamond rush of all time took place in the 19th century. Biodiversity in the nature and game reserves is enormous and a visit to the Kruger National Park, one of the world's largest wildlife conservation areas, is a must. Its moderate sunny climate makes the southernmost tip of Africa an ideal travel destination all year round. October to April are the spring and summer months which are especially appealing to visitors from the northern hemisphere seeking a reprieve from their dreary winters. When

A visit to the Kruger National Park is a must

100 BC The Khoisan people migrated to the south of the continent from central Africa

600 AD The first Bantu tribes settled on the east coast of South Africa

1488 Bartholomew Diaz circum-navigated the Cape of Good Hope

1652 First white settlers under Jan van Riebeeck founded a supply station at the Cape

1658 Arrival of Asian and African slaves

you do the long drive from Johannesburg to Cape Town, and once you have made your way through the final mountain range that separates the Cape from the interior, you will feel as though you have arrived in the Garden of Eden. Stretching before you are vineyards, orchards and fields as far as the eye can see. In the distance one can see the ocean and Cape Town with its unmistakable landmark, Table Mountain. In the valley below you are wine estates where you can can sample wines in a picture-perfect setting. It is worth mentioning that the Atlantic coastline up to Namibia remains largely unspoilt. Namaqualand is renowned for its spring flowers which turn the countryside into a multi-coloured sea of wild flowers from August to October. The Atlantic Ocean can be very cold but the further you head eastwards away from Cape Town along the Indian Ocean, the warmer the sea becomes. The popular Garden Route takes you through Knysna and Plettenberg Bay which forms the first part of this route. It is in the big cities in particular that you will come into contact with the diversity of cultures that is synonymous with South Africa. Durban, the KwaZulu-Natal metropolis is home to the Zulu – one of Africa's proudest tribes – and the next largest group is Asian Indians who make up about 20 per cent. Durban and the KwaZulu-Natal north coast are popular holiday destinations due to the year round mild tropical climate. Further inland you will find the captivating Valley of a Thousand Hills and Drakensberg Mountain range – its highest peak Mont-aux-

A picture-perfect landscape

- 1688 Arrival of the French Huguenots
- 1795 British occupation of the Cape
- 1814 Boer rebellion against British rule
- 1815 Shaka became Zulu king
- 1835 The Boers began their Great Trek north
- 1838 Battle of Blood River between Boers and Zulus
- 1867 Discovery of first diamond

Sources lies 3299m (10823ft) above sea level and is part of the spectacular panorama that awaits you in the Royal Natal National Park. Then there are the beaches between Mtubatuba and the Mozambican border that are particularly beautiful. In contrast to the lush green KwaZulu-Natal with its abundant rain, there is the Free State and the Northern Province, both of which rely on summer rains and revert to a dry and dusty landscape in winter. It is at this time of year that Africa is at its most impressive. Sunshine during the day juxtaposed by night temperatures that can drop by up to 20° C (68° F) to temperatures below freezing!

The two largest cities, Tshwane and Johannesburg, have almost merged into one, however each has retained its own distinctive identity. Johannesburg is a fast-paced glitzy financial metropolis. Tshwane is a quiet reflective administrative capital. Sprawling townships and squatter camps still abound on both their peripheries even 18 years after the country's transition to full democracy in 1994. Some are now equipped with water and electricity, an initiative applauded by the United Nations. The state builds thousands of new houses every year but the population figures are on the rise.

The first European settlement was in Cape Town

Cape Town, affectionately referred to as the Mother City, is where European settlement had its beginnings. When the Portuguese seafarer Bartholomew Diaz came upon the Cape of Storms at the end of the 15th century, it was already home to the Khoisan and San Bushmen. The first settlers in the area surrounding Cape Town were from the Netherlands (later known as the Boers) and from Germany and French Huguenots driven out of France for their faith arrived in 1688. They went on to establish South African's viticulture industry. When the English, keen to expand their colonial might, arrived in the Cape and introduced some relatively liberal human rights policies, many of the Boers headed inland in 1835. After a hard fight for freedom Great Britain declared Cape Town a crown colony in 1899. The British and Boers fought bitterly until the beginning of the 20th century when the South African Union was founded in 1910. From 1948 onwards the country became increasingly isolated internationally for its apartheid policies. Crippled by sanctions, the country's turning point came about during the leadership of President FW (Frederik Willem) de Klerk, who took over government in 1989. He released African National Congress (ANC) leader Nelson Mandela after almost 30 years in detention,

1886 Founding of the city of Johannesburg

1910 Merger between British colonies and Boer republic into the South African Union

1948 Apartheid became legislation

1960 Pass law uprisings, 60 dead in Sharpeville

1961 Withdrawal from the Commonwealth

1976 Pupil unrest in Soweto

A Xhosa rondavel village – the epitome of Africa

South Africa – the rainbow nation

abolished all apartheid laws and set the stage for a peaceful transition to democracy. After the first free elections in 1994, Nelson Mandela was voted into power as South African State President. South Africa has since become known as the 'rainbow nation' for its colourful mix of cultures and religions. It has eleven official languages – Zulu, Xhosa, Afrikaans, Northern Sotho, Sesotho, Tswana, Tsonga, Swati, Ndebele, Venda and English – the latter of which has become the country's lingua franca and is predominantly spoken in the cities. There are two capital cities: Pretoria, part of the city of Tshwane, is the seat of government while Cape Town is the parliamentary capital.

'A world in one country – South Africa' is the very apt slogan synonymous with the country.

- **1990** Activist Nelson Mandela released
- **1994** Nelson Mandela voted as president in first free democratic elections
- **2001** South Africa's Peace and Reconciliation Commission submitted its report
- **2009** Jacob Zuma became South Africa's fourth president since full democracy
- **2010** South Africa became the first African country to host the World Cup Soccer championships

WHAT'S HOT

1 Ethno chic

Local design in Jo'burg Nkhensani is the clothing designer and owner of the *Sun Goddess* label. The message her designs send out is that Africa need not only produce ethnic fashion *(54 Siemert Rd, photo)*. Her designs are a blend of ethnic influences and modern design techniques and materials *(Nelson Mandela Sq)* while award-winning *Black Coffee* daringly blends traditional tribal wear with modern influences *(in the Bamboo Centre, 9th St)*.

2 On canvas

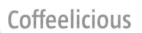

The art scene Offbeat and outlandish best describes South African art. Norman Catherine is one of South Africa's most renowned creative voices and his paintings and sculptures have been well received abroad *(www.normancatherine.co.za, photo)*. His colleague Karen Lasserre's works are characterised by typical African themes that come to life on the canvas in bursts of colour *(www.lasserre.co.za)*. For contemporary South African art visit the *Fried Contemporary Art Gallery (430 Charles St, Pretoria)*.

3 Coffeelicious

Feel good factor Afternoon tea takes on a whole new meaning at *Coffee Cats*, an SPCA associated coffee shop. Here furry friends get to roam freely among guests sipping their Illy coffee and cake *(Willowfield Rd, Durban)*. *The Book Lounge* in Cape Town really lives up to its name. Peruse your favourite book in a relaxed setting while you sip one of the best milkshakes the city has to offer *(71 Roeland St)*. Typically African is *Nzolo Brand Café*, ideal for people watching and for some authentic national fare *(48 Church St, Cape Town)*.

There are a lot of things to discover in South Africa. Here is our hand-picked selection

Into the abyss

4

Kloofing A bathing costume, hiking boots, helmet and sun protection form the basic kit a kloofer will need. Secured with a harness and rope, you will climb down gorges to the cool damp world below and then follow the river crossing boulders and waterfalls. A favourite kloof (the Afrikaans word for ravine), is *Kamikaze Canyon*. If the name is not enough to scare you off then check into Cape Town's *Ashanti Lodge* which also houses the *Ashanti Travel Centre* which organises tours to the canyon *(11 Hof St, www.ashanti.co.za)*. Another excellent operator is *Abseil Africa* in Cape Town's Long Street *(www.abseilafrica.co.za, photo)*. If you prefer to scale a landmark like Table Mountain then *Downhill Adventures (Overbeek Building, Orange St, Cape Town, www.downhilladventures.com)* is for you.

Let me entertain you

5

Spoilt for choice Be it cabaret or comedy clubs, live music or shows, South Africans attach great importance to entertainment. The first point of contact in Cape Town is the *Jou Ma Se Comedy Club.* Performances are in different locations with a changing rota of comedians and quite often it is the club's founder Kurt Schoonraad himself *(www.kurt.co.za)*. *On Broadway* with its dinner cabaret is always on *(44 Long St, photo)*. *Bassline* is the music hot spot in Johannesburg *(10 Henry Nxumalo St)* while in Bloemfontein it is *Die Mystic Boer (84 Kellner St)*.

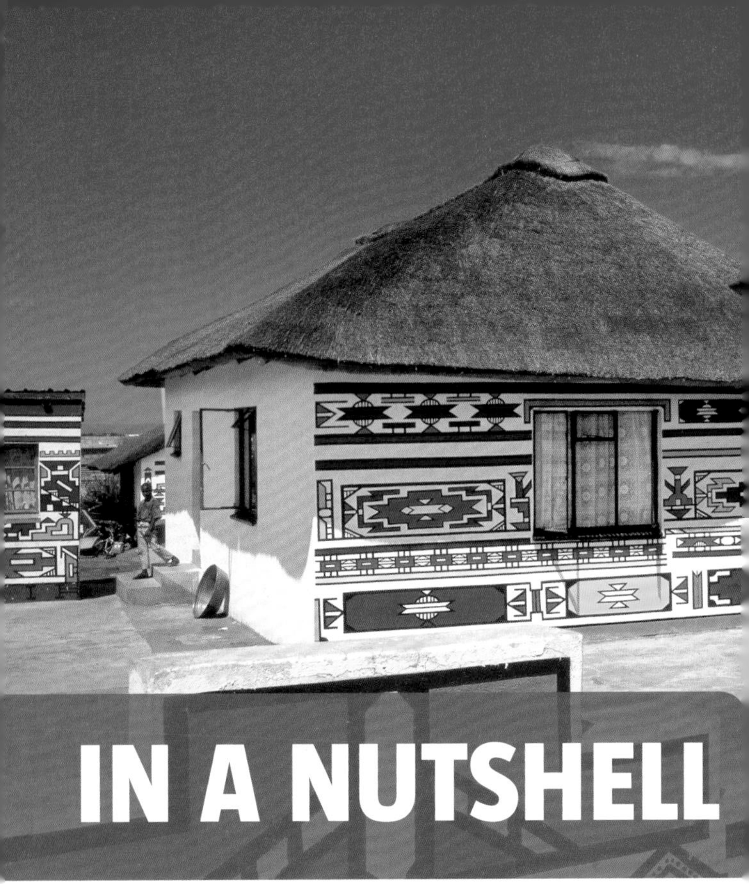

IN A NUTSHELL

AIDS

The number of Aids victims in southern Africa continues to remain high. In South Africa 20 per cent of the adult population is HIV positive. Average life expectancy is 36 years. Aids orphans number in the region of one million. The new head of state, Jacob Zuma, has heralded in a new era of AIDS treatment, however the downside of this has been that HIV/Aids is now being afforded less news coverage.

APARTHEID

The word apartheid is an Afrikaans word that means 'separation'. Apartheid was formalised through a law that separated the races from each other. This enforced racial segregation meant that the majority of South Africa's non-white inhabitants were controlled by a white Afrikaner minority led by the Nationalist government. They upheld this policy of official racial segregation from 1948 until its abolition with the country's transition to full democracy in 1994. The African National Congress (ANC) was formed in 1912 to fight for the rights of the majority of black South Africans. The party fought apartheid and the party now hold the majority in parliament and leads the country.

Photo: Traditional art – Ndebele houses

Back to basics: a few pointers to help you in your quest to get to know and understand some South African idiosyncrasies

ART

The country's oldest art are the San cave paintings going back thousands of years ago. European settlers also brought with them their art traditions. The most famous of the European artists is the 19th century landscape artist Jan Hendrik Pierneef. Today his paintings fetch staggering prices at auctions. Also of European descent is Irma Stern, another of the country's outstanding artists who worked in Cape Town in the 1920s and has a museum dedicated to her. Post apartheid art in South Africa is as diverse as its population with William Kentridge as the contemporary artist currently fetching the highest prices for his works. Township life is depicted in the works of Willie Bester and Vusi Khumalo. All three have made a name for themselves internationally.

BLACK ECONOMIC EMPOWERMENT – BEE

Black participation in the economy is a pragmatic growth strategy that aims to realise the country's full economic potential while helping to bring the black majority into the full economic mainstream. BEE opens up management positions and partnership portfolios for those previously disadvantaged. Although not enforced by law, many firms uphold it in order to have the benefit of being able to do business with government.

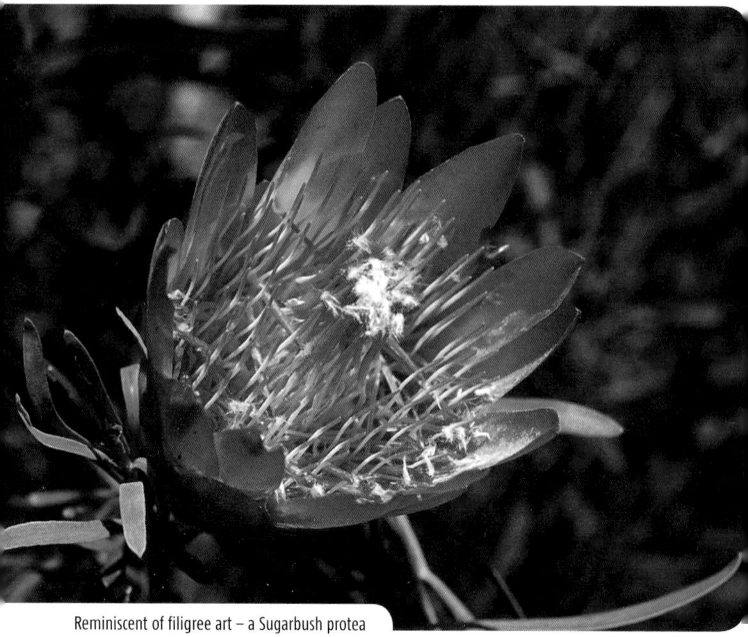

Reminiscent of filigree art – a Sugarbush protea

ECONOMY

Mining is considered one of the country's most important economic sectors – aside from agriculture – and accounts for the biggest job creation. South Africa is the world's leading gold producer, supplying 50 per cent of world demand. It is also one of the largest diamond suppliers. Every year some 1.2 million tons of fish is caught in its oceans and of this 90 per cent is exported. Tourism is the third largest source of foreign exchange earnings. In the past two decades, investments as well as profits have seen a steady increase with thousands of employment and training opportunities being created.

In the past few years a flourishing film industry has developed in Cape Town. International commercials and even Hollywood blockbusters are filmed here.

Despite the economic upturn and successful financial policies instituted by the government there are still many unemployed South Africans. This figure is estimated to be 30 per cent of the employable population. The government has implemented an affirmative action programme which affords previously disadvantaged South Africans with equal qualifications greater opportunities.

FLORA

The region's different climatic zones make it home to an exceptionally diverse floral kingdom of more than 23,000 species. South Africa's national flower, the protea, has 400 known varieties. Kirstenbosch in Cape Town is the place to view them in the spring *(www.sanbi.org)*.
Six floral kingdoms – where all members of one plant species grow within the border of a country – have been identified worldwide and the Western Cape is one of these. Here all 6552 species of the fynbos family flourish, including proteas and ericas.

HOMELAND

The homeland system was a policy of the apartheid system enforced by the National Party. In order to further separate the races the homeland initiative created ten so-called 'independent' states or homelands within South Africa. The states were based on ethnic identities and these states within a state made up a mere 13 per cent of the country but had to contain a full 80 per cent of the population. There was hardship and extreme poverty in the homelands as they were unable to develop their local economies. Today these areas have once again been incorporated into South Africa but it will take some time for the apartheid legacy to disappear.

NELSON MANDELA

After 27 years in jail, the then 70 year-old Nelson Mandela was freed from prison in 1990. During the apartheid era he was an anti-apartheid activist and the iconic leader of the banned resistance movement, the African National Congress. With his accession to presidency in 1994 South Africa made the peaceful transition to full mulit-racial democracy.
In 1993 Mandela received the Nobel Peace Prize together with South Africa's last National Party president FW de Klerk. He held the office of South African president from 1994 to 1999 after having been

POST WORLD CUP SOUTH AFRICA

Not only was the 2010 World Cup Soccer a resounding success for the sport but also for the country. South Africans were very proud that the new stadiums were completed on time, that there was very little serious crime during the event and that everything ran smoothly. The nation stood together and people of all colours celebrated the success of the games. At the time the country's infrastructure received a considerable boost, its airports were refurbished (or newly built like the one in Durban), a new high speed train, the Gautrain went into operation in Johannesburg and special bus lanes were introduced in other cities. The fears of sceptics who predicted that the World Cup stadiums (five of them brand new and five revamped) would become white elephants have been unfounded. Johannesburg's massive Soccer City stadium has already paid for itself after only a year thanks to bookings by international performers like U2, while the rest are well on their way to achieving the same.

elected in the country's first democratic elections. He withdrew from office and politics after his term and unlike many other African countries, South Africa has already had its third elected president. In South Africa he is often referred to affectionately as Madiba, which is his Xhosa clan name.

POPULATION

South Africa's official population figure has passed the 50 million mark. The majority of the population, with 77 per cent, is black. The white and coloured population are estimated to be 11 per cent white and 9 per cent respectively, while the Indian/Asian population is estimated to be 3 per cent – the latter as a result of the 19th century influx of sugar plantation workers to KwaZulu-Natal. Reliable sources also put a figure of an additional 4 million undocumented immigrants – made up of Zimbabweans and illegal refugees from the rest of Africa. There are eleven official languages spoken. The Khoisan tribes are regarded as the earliest residents of the country – among them were the Khoikhoi (who were almost completely wiped out) and the San Bushmen. Dwindling numbers of these nomadic people still live in the Kalahari Desert just as their ancestors have done for thousands of years; cave paintings bear testimony to their history. The Zulu consider Zululand in KwaZulu-Natal as their native land while the Xhosa tribes can be traced back to Umtata (in the Eastern Cape region) as far back as the 15th century.

The Afrikaner people are descendants of the Dutch, German and French and their unique language is a blend of Dutch with some German, French and Malay influences. The English speakers are descendants of British settlers who come to the country from the late 18th century onwards.

RENAMING OF CITIES

As soon as the new South Africa came into being, many of the province's names were changed e.g. the southern Transvaal became Gauteng. City names have also been affected e.g. Pietersburg is now called Polokwane. The old names still appear on some traffic signs together with the new ones. Cities are also in the process of renaming their streets.

SAFETY & SECURITY

It is worth mentioning that the police have taken serious measures to combat crime over the past few years and city centres like Cape Town and Johannesburg are now under constant CCTV surveillance. Stick to the unwritten rules as you would in any other country where there are large differences in wealth. Never wear cameras and expensive jewellery openly and take extra care at ATMs. Taking a walk along a deserted street at night is an absolute no-no.

SPORT

South Africans love their sport – be it as active participants or observers. They jog, swim and cycle and sport plays a prominent role in the schools with rugby and/or cricket and football (since the World Cup) becoming increasingly popular among male pupils. Female pupils go for hockey, netball or volleyball.

If a South African national team – irrespective of the sport – is successful internationally the whole country backs them. Sport as a uniting force is something that Nelson Mandela promoted during his presidency. In the 1990s he brought the Rugby World Cup to South Africa and famously wore the team jersey when he handed the captain of the then predominantly white team the winning trophy. This sporting event is credited with having brought about greater unity in South Africa than many political actions. This sense of unity once again manifested itself when the country successfully hosted the 2010 Soccer World Cup.

personal with the wildlife. Private game reserves can be quite pricy but it is worth bearing in mind that private conservation efforts can be very expensive.

Tracking wildlife in a game reserve in an open vehicle

TOWNSHIP

This is the designation given to the segregation of city suburbs into black, coloured and Indian residential areas prior to the country's transition to full democracy in 1994. The 'borders' were fuzzy at best and today the term is used predominantly to define the sprawling suburbs inhabited by poorer South Africans.

WILDLIFE

The biodiversity prevalent in South Africa's game reserves is unrivalled in the world. Visitors can drive through the state-run national parks in their own closed vehicles while private reserves have qualified rangers with open off-road vehicles – a unique opportunity to get up close and

The largest and most sought after game reserve is the Kruger National Park. It is home to large numbers of the Big Five – buffalo, elephant, leopard, lion and rhino. Today private game reserves are also located inside the Kruger National Park. During the apartheid area these areas were cleared of people in order to extend the park, they have now been returned to their original inhabitants.
South Africa has always been exemplary when it comes to nature conservation and this policy now also forms part of its new constitution. In the past few years cross-border Transfrontier Parks have been established between South Africa and Namibia and between South Africa, Zimbabwe and Mozambique.

FOOD & DRINK

There is no single definition of what constitutes authentic South African cuisine. Specialities tend to be regional. Cape cuisine has been strongly influenced by Malaysian cooking while fiery Indian curries and chutneys are the hallmarks of KwaZulu-Natal's cuisine.

South Africans love to *braai* (a South African barbecue) which is more of a social event than a culinary experience. Prime cuts of marinated steak, spiced spare ribs, kebabs, seasoned lamb and pork chops and boerewors – a highly seasoned sausage – are what a *braai* is all about. The barbecued meat is served with *stywe pap,* a polenta-style maize dish. The African way to eat it is to mould the *pap* into a ball with your hands and dunk it in the gravy. On weekends South Africans from all walks of life get together to *braai*. The men stand around the fire with their beers in hand while the women catch up on their news while they prepare the accompanying salads.

Most restaurants have a wide variety of fish on their menus – freshly caught in the coastal regions. Seafood like mussels, oysters and squid and fish like kingklip, snoek and yellowtail are usually found on restaurant menus but it is also a good idea to try the more seasonal catch of the day in the restaurants on the coastal regions.

Photo: Ostrich steak

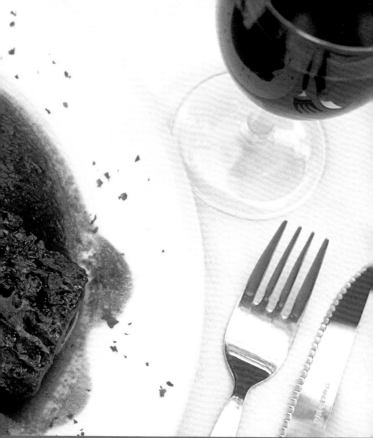

A gourmet feast awaits the visitor with a dizzying array of Asian, Indian, European and local cuisine to tantalise the taste buds

There are also several popular outdoor beach restaurants that serve grilled fish straight from the sea. *Crayfish* is a shellfish that is combination between lobster and langoustine. This delicacy costs a fraction of the price you would pay for it back home. Fruit and vegetables are available in abundance and the quality is excellent. Produce is grown almost exclusively in the open air and you can taste the difference in the flavour and quality of the products. Grapes, melons and apples are highly recommended. Unique to the Cape are the Cape gooseberries. The small yellow fruits are used for cakes and jams. *Waterblommetjies* grow on many ponds from May. They are indigenous water hyacinths that only grow in the Cape and are a sought after ingredient for the local dish *waterblommetjie bredie*, a lamb stew.

LOCAL SPECIALITIES

▶ **Biltong** – this popular snack is air dried fillet of beef or game usually sliced very thinly. It originated during the Great Trek when the Boers needed to preserve their meat for their epic cross country journey

▶ **Bobotie** – a curried lamb mince casserole spiced with dried apricots and raisins or sultanas, topped with an egg and milk mixture and then baked. Served with saffron rice and garnished with chutney. This dish has its origins in the Cape Malay community

▶ **Bredie** – or a South African stew or casserole usually made with mutton and vegetables often with a tomato base and seasoned with cinnamon and cardamom. The *waterblommetjie bredie* is made with the flowers of the Cape water lily (photo left)

▶ **Droëwors** – Afrikaans for 'dried sausage', it also has its origins in the Great Trek where thin, well spiced sausages were air dried for the long journey

▶ **Isibindi** – thinly sliced lamb liver with onions

▶ **Kingklip** – a popular South African saltwater fish and a member of the cod family, usually served as a fillet

▶ **Koeksisters** – very sweet and sticky, a plaited dough delicacy that is deep fried and dunked in syrup before serving

▶ **Pap** – a maize porridge (similar to polenta) that the Afrikaans community calls pap and eats with *sous* (a tomato and onion sauce) but that actually has its origins in the black African diet where it is called *putu* and is served with *amasi* (a sauce made of sour milk)

▶ **Perlemon** – also called abalone is a large shellfish found in the Atlantic Ocean

▶ **Potjiekos** – a dish of potatoes, meat and vegetables stacked in layers in a cast iron potjie that will stew over an open fire for up to five hours

▶ **Samoosa** – small, triangular deep fried strongly spiced pastry parcels stuffed with a vegetable or meat filling (photo right)

▶ **Sosaties** – kebabs of lamb, dried fruit, tomatoes and onions usually flame grilled

▶ **Sousboontjies** – dried beans cooked together with butter, sugar, vinegar and other vegetables

▶ **Ulusu** – tripe boiled until tender in a sauce of onions, celery and potatoes

You can safely drink tap water wherever you go as South Africa's water quality ranks among the world's best, one of the reasons why bottled water has only recently become popular. Beer is also one of the most popular alcoholic beverages along with cocktails and spirits like vodka and whiskey.

Even though the country has been producing wine for more than 300 years it has only been in the last few decades that it has become an integral part of the lifestyle of many South Africans. The conditions for viticulture are perfect and South African wines are excellent, the Cape wine lands are a paradise for wine lovers.

If you start your trip in the Cape you should do the Franschhoek, Stellenbosch, Paarl or Constantia wine routes. Wine tasting is offered on most estates so you will soon be able to decide on your favourite wine selection for your evening meals. Some recommended estates are: *Meerlust, Hamilton Russell, Springfield, Simonsig, Bouchard Finlayson, Waterford* and *Tokara.* Pinotage – a red varietal that is a cross between Pinot Noir and Cinsaut – is unique to South Africa and comes highly recommended.

When ordering a cup of coffee, first check it is filter coffee and avoid disappointment as there are still some areas (mostly small towns in the interior) where instant coffee is still used. For the adventurous palate why not try *rooibos* tea, produced from the fine needle-like leaves of an indigenous bush that only grows in the Cedarberg.

You will find a large selection of restaurants especially in the big cities and the holiday resort areas. South Africa's cuisine is international and there is hardly a nationality that is not represented by a restaurant. If you enjoy a bottle of wine or a beer with your meal then it is worth making sure that the restaurant you choose has a liquor license. Be aware that a distinction is

The South African climate is ideal for grape cultivation

also made between a full liquor license and one that only permits the serving of wine and beer. If a restaurant is unlicensed you can bring your own drinks. Normally a restaurant will advise you that it is not licensed when you book a table.

Restaurants are generally open for lunch between noon and 2.30pm and between 7pm and 11pm for evening meals. In rural areas many restaurants remain closed on Mondays and often also on a Sunday evening. You should always reserve a table for evening meals especially in the main cities. It is also worth noting that some restaurants and hotels have an evening dress code.

In South Africa smoking is prohibited in all public buildings but certain restaurants have smokers' sections.

SHOPPING

Souvenirs from South Africa are exotic, artistic and varied. Finding exactly the right memento to take home for yourself or a gift for family or friends can be a daunting task: richly embellished clothing, jewellery, wooden carvings and every conceivable craft will leave you spoilt for choice. Then there are the shopping malls that are the hallmark of every city and town. They often have more 100 stores per mall and they have everything the heart desires under one (air conditioned!) roof.

ARTS & CRAFTS

Many indigenous tribes have an affinity for beadwork and create stunning works of art that also often convey an important message. The Zulu and Xhosa for example, will send love letters in the form of small beaded messages that hang from safety pins.

The Zulu make material dolls, birds from pine cones and calabash bowls from pumpkins. White and orange are typical colours used for Xhosa garments and bags, always embroidered with beads. The Ndebele on the other hand are renowned for their leather loincloths. Also available are Ndebele dolls in traditional garb that embody fertility and masculinity. In some stores the profits from the sale of traditional arts and crafts go to charitable causes. In Cape Town: *Wola Nani, Unit 3, Block A, Collingwood Place, 9 Drake St, www.wolanani.co.za;* in Knysna: *The Muse Factory, The Old Goal Complex, 17 Queen St;* in Durban: *Woza Moya, 26 Old Main Rd;* in Johannesburg: *Kunye, Garden Shop, 278 Main Rd*

CARVINGS

Here you need to be careful as a lot of what is on offer is mass produced in factories in neighbouring countries. If it is authentic art that you are after then it is best to get advice from a specialised dealer.

JEWELLERY

The price of gold and diamonds in South Africa does not differ from that of other countries as they are determined by the international market. It is however worth buying jewellery here for the authentic

Beads, jewellery and so much more: South Africa has a wide selection of sophisticated arts and crafts on offer

South African craftsmanship. The quality is excellent and the prices reasonable. Only buy from dealers certified by the Jewellery Council of South Africa.

OSTRICH LEATHER

The range is endless: handbags, briefcases, suitcases, wallets, shoes etc. are all produced from this large bird's hide. It can be difficult to differentiate between originals and knock-offs so only buy leather goods at speciality stores. A rule of thumb: the fewer the nodules, the more expensive the leather. The smoother leather comes from the bird's legs and is not as valuable.

SAFARI OUTFITS

It is definitely best to kit yourself out for the great outdoors when you arrive in South Africa. Not only is it far cheaper than back home but the quality is excellent. Your best bet is the *Cape Union Mart* chain *(www.capeunionmart.co.za)*. Most large malls have an outlet.

WINE

South Africa is a veritable paradise for wine connoisseurs. Many of its wine estates offer wine tasting and will ship your purchases home for you – important to bear this in mind as you are only permitted to take two bottles through customs when you leave the country. A premium bottle of wine can set you back 100 rand but even a cheap 25 rand bottle will be decent enough. A good idea is to refer to the John Platter Wine Guide *(www.wineonaplatter.com)* which gives an overview of all the estates and rates their wines. You can buy a copy at most bookshops and stationery outlets.

THE PERFECT ROUTE

MODERN METROPOLIS AND CULTURAL VILLAGE

1 *Johannesburg* → p. 83 is a city abuzz with boundless energy and drive, multiple lane motorways and wild motorists, skyscrapers and sprawling townships. This, the commercial capital of Africa, is the perfect place to start your road trip. As soon as you leave the outskirts of this megacity and head north on the R 26 you will have the great expanse of Africa ahead of you. Three hours later you will reach the 2 *Golden Gate Highlands National Park* → p. 70 where imposing sandstone cliffs shimmer golden in the sunlight. Pay a visit to the 3 *Basotho Cultural Village* → p. 70 where members still live as they did 100 years ago.

ARTISTS' VILLAGE AND TRADITIONAL KINGDOM

A few kilometres on you will reach the village of 4 *Clarens* → p. 70. It has become very popular over the past few years among people seeking an alternative lifestyle. Be sure to set aside enough time for a visit to a few art galleries followed by a delicious lunch at Clementine's. Continue your journey on the R 26 to 5 *Ladybrand* → p. 71, a town on the border of 6 *Lesotho* → p. 71 which is also known as the 'kingdom in the sky' (photo left).

RURAL TOWNS AND NATIONAL PARKS

The R 701 takes you to the country's largest dam. The 7 *Gariep Dam* → p. 33 has become popular with international windsurfers for its ideal conditions. *Forever Resorts* right by the water's edge is your best bet for an overnight stay. Continue your journey on the R 390 in the direction of 8 *Cradock* → p. 37, a small town with a number of renovated Victorian homes where you have to stop for a drink at the *Victoria Hotel*. Pass the 9 *Mountain Zebra National Park* → p. 38 (photo right) and you will reach 10 *Graaff-Reinet* → *p. 36* and at *Gordon's Restaurant* you can treat yourself to their excellent lamb dish. Before continuing with the journey, pay a visit to 11 *Camdeboo National Park's* → p. 37 *Valley of Desolation* to see its impressive rock formations.

THE KAROO

Continue on the N 9 until a right turn takes you on the R 341 to the town of 12 *Oudtshoorn* → p. 36 the capital of the ostrich farming region. Visit

Experience multi-faceted South Africa with a journey from Johannesburg to Cape Town

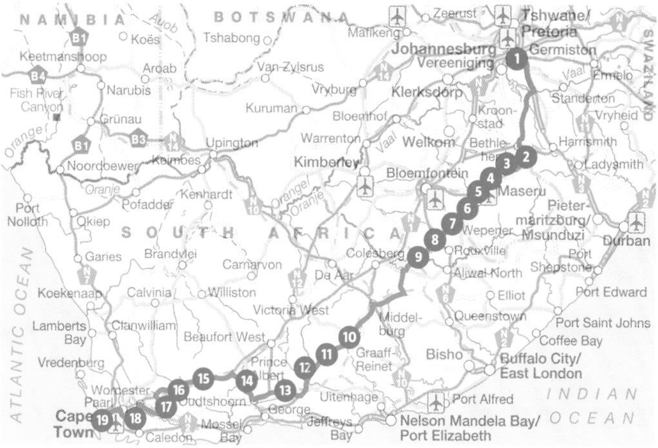

one of the ostrich farms and sample an ostrich egg omelette. Next, the R 328 will take you over one of the country's most impressive mountain passes to ⓭ ***Prince Albert***, a sleepy Karoo village with enchanting hotels and guest houses perfect for an overnight stop. Continue your trip on the N 1 national road. After three hours you will reach ⓮ ***Montagu***.

WINE ESTATES AND THE MOTHER CITY

From here take the R 60 via ⓯ ***Worcester*** → p. 94 until it veers left to the R 43. Continue on the R 43 via ⓰ ***Villiersdorp*** → p. 94 situated on the ⓱ ***Theewaterskloof Dam*** → p. 94 and pass through the Elephant Pass with its spectacular view of the Franschhoek valley. Two excellent restaurants *La Petite Ferme* and *Haute Cabrière* are located along the route. ⓲ ***Franschhoek*** → p. 58 is right in the heart of the Cape wine lands and is considered to be South Africa's culinary capital. From here the R 45 takes you past the wine estates and just before you get to the motorway on-ramp in the direction of Cape Town you will come across one of the country's oldest wine estates: *Babylonstoren*. Continue on the N 1 for another half an hour and you will finally reach ⓳ ***Cape Town*** → p. 49, South Africa's oldest city, the *Mother City*.

1400km (870mi). Driving time: 18 hours. Recommended duration of journey: one week. Detailed map of the route on the back cover, in the road atlas and the pull-out map

CAPE PROVINCES

The Cape provinces comprise 60 per cent of the country's surface area and offers some rather extreme contrasts. From the dry Kalahari Desert in the north to the dense forests of the Garden Route in the east and in the centre, the semi-desert Karoo. Some may find the isolation of the Karoo intimidating; others will see it as a place of silence and solace.

One of the main attractions is the ★ ● *Garden Route* along the Indian Ocean – it extends from the small industrial town of Mossel Bay to the mouth of the Storms River. The climate is mild all year round. The MARCO POLO Cape Town travel guide will have more in-depth information.

The west coast of the Cape is much drier and more rugged than the *Garden Route*. The resort town of *Langebaan* with its lagoon is reminiscent of the Mediterranean while the interior here opens up into desert-like *Namaqualand* which transforms into a sea of wild flowers between August and October after the rains. The *Vanrhyns Pass* in the Northern Cape is the best vantage point from which to view this spectacular sight.

Even further in the north lies the fascinating Kalahari Desert and the *Kgalagadi Transfrontier National Park.* Stretching across a huge section of South Africa and Namibia, there are no border fences and

Photo: Knysna Heads

Desert and lush greenery: be it barren wilderness or idyllic forests, each landscape has its own special appeal

the game can move freely, as can tourists. The dramatic *Augrabies* waterfalls are at their awe-inspiring best when the Gariep River floods and huge volumes of water plunge some 56m (183ft) into the ravine. Port Elizabeth, today part of the Nelson Mandela Bay municipality, is the capital of the Eastern Cape. The province is home to the Xhosa tribe to which Nelson Mandela belongs. A few kilometres on is the *Addo Elephant Park*, home to elephants and as well as a number of other wild animals.

GEORGE

(127 E5) (*🕮 F8*) **The capital of the Garden Route (pop. of 200,000) it lies at the foot of the Outeniqua Mountains and is surrounded by an idyllic park-like landscape.**

Cango Caves – unique and impressive stalactite caves near Oudtshoorn

Travelling from the interior, you reach George via the Montagu or Outeniqua Passes. Once in the city itself take a stroll along its high street, *York Street* and visit some of its old bookstores. One of the old oaks on the street is the *Old Slave Tree* which is a national monument that marks the spot where slaves were traded. Also worth a visit is *St Mark's Cathedral*, Africa's smallest cathedral.

SIGHTSEEING

GARDEN ROUTE BOTANICAL GARDEN

Plants unique to the Garden Route are grown over an area of 30 acres. *49 Caledon St | Mon–Thu 8am–5pm, Fri 8am–2.30pm | admission free*

GEORGE MUSEUM

Once a courthouse, now a museum where visitors can learn all about the local timber industry. *Old Drostdy Building | Courtenay St | Mon–Fri 9am–4.45pm, Sat 9am–12.30pm | admission free*

OUTENIQUA CHOO TJOE

The ride in this old steam locomotive takes you to Mossel Bay. *Mon, Wed and Fri 10am from George and 2.15pm from Mossel Bay, duration of journey almost three hours | tel. 04 48 01 82 88 | tickets 110 rand | at time of press closed due to flood damage*

FOOD & DRINK

KAFE SEREFÉ

Located right in the heart of the city, this bistro is popular not only for its successful fusion of Turkish and South African dishes but also for its top quality meat. *Corner Courtenay St/Ironside St | tel. 04 48 84 10 12 | Budget*

OLD TOWNHOUSE
Traditional dishes are the hallmark of this restaurant located in one of the city's oldest buildings. *Corner York St/Market St | tel. 04 48 74 36 63 | Moderate*

SPORTS & ACTIVITIES

Eight exceptional golf courses make George South Africa's golfing Mecca *(find out more from George Tourism)* while *Victoria Bay* is a world famous surf destination. The INSIDER TIP Silverspray B & B *(4 rooms | tel. 08 25 12 18 48 | www.silverspray.co.za | Budget)* lies just 6m (20ft) from the sea.

WHERE TO STAY

FANCOURT ★ ● ☺
This impressive country estate dating back to 1860 has three golf courses, indoor and outdoor swimming pools and a marvellous garden. Fancourt has been praised for its water conservation measures in the maintenance of its golf courses. *86 rooms | Montagu St | tel. 04 48 04 00 00 | www.fancourt.com | Expensive*

GARDENVILLA
This romantic B & B lies at the foot of the Quteniqua Mountains surrounded by an acre of garden. *5 rooms | 35 Plantation Rd | tel. 04 48 74 03 91 | www.gardenvilla.co.za | Budget*

INFORMATION

GEORGE TOURISM
124 York St | tel. 04 48 01 91 03 | www.visitgeorge.co.za

WHERE TO GO

CANGO CAVES ★ (127 E5) *(F8)*
These underground caves some 80km (50mi) north-west of George are among the world's most fascinating stalagmite and stalactite caves. For more than 20 million years rainwater has been corroding the limestone, leading to the formation of massive hollows and tunnels. Expect to be awed by the unique interplay of shapes and colours. *Guided tours (60 or 90 minutes) on the hour or half hour from 9am to 4pm | entrance fee 64–80 rand*

MARCO POLO HIGHLIGHTS

★ Garden Route
South Africa's famous coastal route along the Indian Ocean
→ p. 32

★ Fancourt
Luxury hotel in the middle of three 18-hole golf courses
→ p. 35

★ Cango Caves
A unique and rare wonder of nature – stalagmite and stalactite caves formed over millions of years – near Oudtshoorn
→ p. 35

★ Kgalagadi Transfrontier Park
Lions and antelopes and much more in this exceptionally beautiful African game park
→ p. 40

★ West Coast National Park
Vast wetland conservation area that is home to many endangered bird species → p. 44

★ Addo Elephant National Park
Visitors are delighted by the sight of elephant calves
→ p. 47

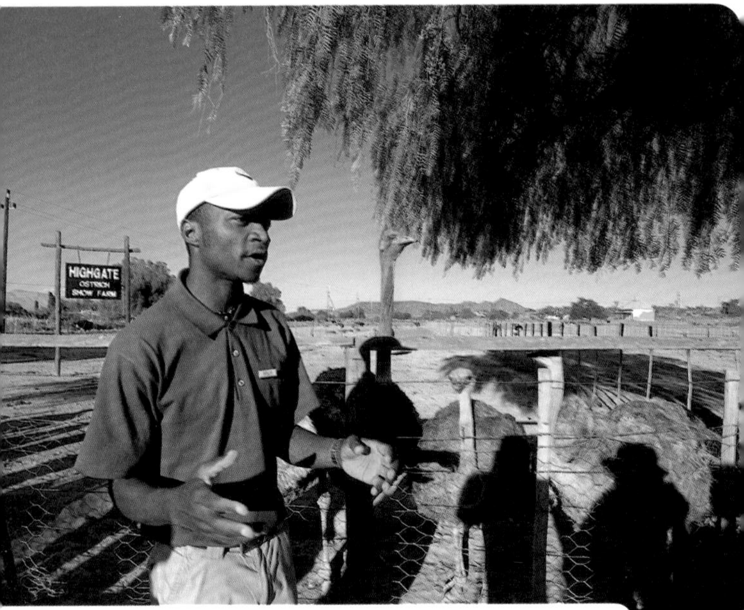

In the know – a guide gives the lowdown on ostrich breeding at the Cango Ostrich Farm

OUDTSHOORN (127 E5) (*🕮 F8*)
Oudtshoorn is the centre of the ostrich farming community. Located 70km (43mi) from George it is the world's most successful ostrich farming area. The farms produce feathers (plucked every nine months) and ostrich leather. Some of the farms offer guided tours e.g. ● *Cango Ostrich Farm (tel. 04 42 72 46 23 | entrance fee 56 rand)*. For an insight into the history of ostrich breeding visit the *C. P. Nel Museum (3 Baron von Rheede St Mon–Fri 8am–5pm, Sat 9am–1pm | entrance fee 16 rand)*. En route to the Cango Caves is the stylish *Altes Landhaus* hotel *(9 rooms | tel. 04 42 72 61 12 | www.alteslandhaus.co.za | Moderate)*.

WILDERNESS (127 E5) (*🕮 F8*)
The town of Wilderness is located at the mouth of the Kaaiman River. Its 5km (3mi) long beach makes this a popular holiday choice. The best hotel in the area is INSIDER TIP *Views (18 rooms |South St | tel. 04 48 77 80 00 www.viewshotel.co.za | Expensive)* which is set high up above the beach and has spectacular ocean views. *Eden Adventures (tel. 04 48 77 01 79 | www.eden.co.za)* organises canoe rides on the Wilderness lagoon and through the national park.

GRAAFF-REINET

(127 F4) (*🕮 G7*) **Surrounded by the Camdeboo National Park, Graaff-Reinet (population of 80,000) is often referred to as the 'jewel of the Karoo'. Founded in 1786, it is one of South Africa's oldest towns.**

The city centre feels like a large outdoor museum with architecture spanning the past 200 years. From simple Karoo huts through to stately Cape Dutch homes (replicas of homes built in Amsterdam in the 18th century) to Victorian cottages, all beautifully restored.

SIGHTSEEING

REINET HOUSE MUSEUM

An extensive collection of Cape Dutch furniture and household utensils, as well as bicycles. The grapevine in front of the building was planted in 1870 and is thought to be the oldest in the country. *Murray St | Mon–Fri 8am–5pm, Sat 9am–5pm, Sun 9am–4pm | entrance fee 20 rand*

FOOD & DRINK

GORDON'S RESTAURANT

For excellent Karoo cuisine, try the highly commended slow roast Karoo lamb. *100 Cradock St | tel. 04 98 92 45 75 | Moderate*

SHOPPING

WINDMILL JUNCTION

From antiquities and art to bric-a-brac and kitsch, owner Amori has an eclectic mix of goods to choose from. *52 Somerset St*

ENTERTAINMENT

The town's two pubs are both at the Drostdy Hotel (the nicest building in town) where you will be able to rub shoulders with Karoo farmers.

WHERE TO STAY

BUITEN VERWAGTEN

This guest house is surrounded by a huge garden and lives up to its name which means 'beyond expectation' and is home to the town's second-oldest grapevine. *5 rooms | 59 Burke St | tel. 04 98 92 45 04 | Budget*

KAMBRO COTTAGE

Although it is located in the middle of town, this small B & B will offer you a quiet and relaxed stay. *4 rooms | 73 Somerset St | tel. 04 98 91 03 60 | kambrocottage@gmail.com | Budget*

INFORMATION

TOURIST INFORMATION BUREAU

13 A Church St | tel. 04 98 92 42 48 | www.graaffreinet.co.za

WHERE TO GO

INSIDER TIP CAMDEBOO NATIONAL PARK (127 F4) (*G7*)

The national park's main attraction is the *Valley of Desolation*, a series of dramatic and sheer cliff faces that stand sentry over an isolated valley. This area is a real force of nature, one that feels suspended in time *(daily from sunrise to sunset | entrance fee 48 rand)*. Stay over at the *Mount Camdeboo Private Game Reserve (11 rooms | tel. 04 98 91 05 70 | www.mountcamdeboo.com | Moderate | 6km (3.7mi) from Graaff-Reinet*

CRADOCK (128 A5) (*H7*)

Cradock is a small very typical Karoo town. South African author Olive Schreiner wrote her 1883 classic, 'The Story of an African Farm' here and the *Olive Schreiner House (9 Cross St)* commemorates her life. 25 Victorian houses in Market Street have been extensively refurbished to form part of the small hotel INSIDER TIP *Die Tuishuise (36 Market St | tel. 04 88 81 13 22 | www.tuishuise.co.za | Budget)*. *100km (62mi) from Graaff-Reinet*

MOUNTAIN ZEBRA NATIONAL PARK

(128 A4) (🗺 H7)

This national park was established in 1937 to prevent the extinction of the Cape Mountain Zebra. When it first opened it had only four animals, today the figures exceed 300. *(Information tel. 04 88 81 24 27 | sanparks.org.za/parks/mountain_zebra | entrance fee 108 rand). 170km (105mi) from Graaff-Reinet*

KIMBERLEY

(128 A2) (🗺 G–H5) **In 1866 a small child found a glistening stone along the banks of the Gariep River and set in motion the biggest diamond rush of all times.**

800m (2642ft) deep – the Big Hole of Kimberly

This discovery laid the foundations of the diamond city Kimberley. Eureka – the first diamond to be found – was 21.75 carats. A replica is on display in the mine museum. Initially the prospectors only searched the river banks but as more and more arrived from around the world, the search expanded away from the river into the earth itself. At first Kimberley (population of 180,000) was little more than a tent city known by the diggers as *New Rush.* By 1870 some 30,000 people were digging for diamonds in the so-called *Big Hole*, the world's largest man-made excavation. It is 800m (2642ft) deep, has a diameter of 1.6km (1mi) and covers an area of 42 acres. 43 years of mining (that ended in 1914) yielded 2722kg (6000lb) of diamonds equivalent to 13.6million carats. The tent city developed into a small city named Kimberley in 1873.

SIGHTSEEING

BIG HOLE AND KIMBERLEY MINE MUSEUM ●

Today a viewing platform spans the crater of the Big Hole. The old part of the city is an open air museum of historical houses. The *Visitors' Centre* depicts the history of the diamond rush and uncut diamonds are displayed in the *Diamond Vault*, among them the famous '616', a 616 carat diamond crystal. *Bulfontein St | 8am–5pm daily | the museum is free, the Big Hole entrance fee is 55 rand*

MCGREGOR MUSEUM

Cecil Rhodes built it as a sanatorium but today the museum not only showcases the lifestyles of the wealthy diamond magnates of the 19th century, but is also home to some major natural and cultural history collections. More displays in *Rudd House* which is next door. *Atlas St | Mon–Sat 9am–5pm, Sun 2–5pm | entrance 15 rand*

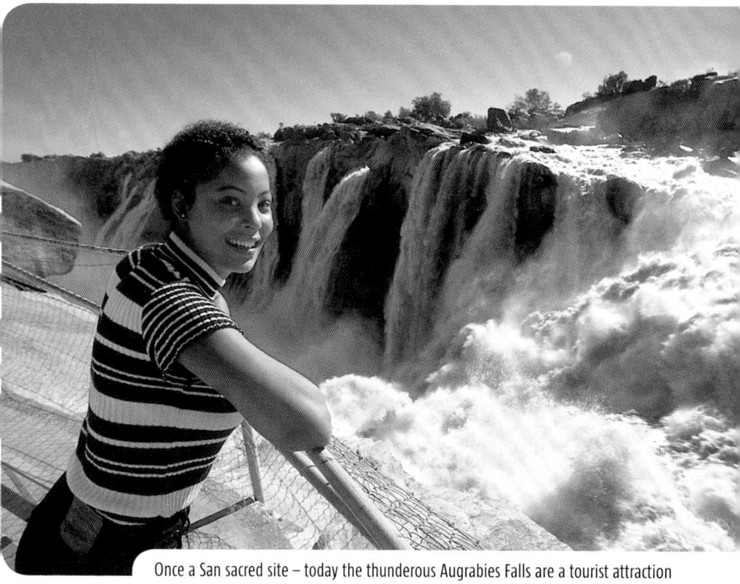

Once a San sacred site – today the thunderous Augrabies Falls are a tourist attraction

FOOD & DRINK

BUTLER'S RESTAURANT

International cuisine is served in a traditional atmosphere in the restaurant situated in the Estate Private Hotel restaurant. *7 Lodge St | tel. 05 38 32 26 68 |* Moderate

WHERE TO STAY

CECIL RHODES GUEST HOUSE

Guests here are transported back in time to the diamond rush era but the amenities are all very modern. *7 rooms | 138 Du Toitspan Rd | tel. 05 38 30 25 00 | www.ceciljohnrhodes.co.za |* Budget

INSIDER TIP PROTEA HOTEL KIMBERLEY

Stylish new hotel built right by the Big Hole. Cocktails served on the patio giving you an awesome view deep into the crater. *94 rooms | West Circular Rd | tel. 05 38 02 82 00 | www.proteahotels.com |* Moderate

INFORMATION

TOURIST INFORMATION OFFICE

Diamantveld Visitor Centre | Tucker Rd | tel. 05 38 32 72 98 | www.kimberley.co.za

WHERE TO GO

AUGRABIES FALLS

(126 C1) (*E5*)

These impressive waterfalls were sacred to the San. They plunge 130m (426ft) into a rock pool and rumour has it that there are diamonds at the bottom of the pool. Any attempts at diving for them would however be futile due to the force of the water *(7.30am–sunset daily | entrance 180 rand)*. The *Dundi Lodge* 3km (1.8mi) from the falls is your INSIDER TIP best bet for an overnight stay in this area *(11 rooms | tel. 05 44 51 92 00 | www.dundilodge.co.za |* Moderate*). Some 400km (248mi) west of Kimberley*

KGALAGADI TRANSFRONTIER NATIONAL PARK ★

(122–123 C–D 2–4) (*E–F 2–3*)
The reserve is the world's largest and most pristine ecosystem. Together with the Botswana National Park it covers an area 4.9 million acres and is home to lions, leopards and antelopes. Three camps offer cottages and bungalows for overnight stays *(B 3 via Upington in the direction of Botswana). 350km (217mi) north-west of Kimberley*

Gemsbok in the Kgalagadi Transfrontier Park

INSIDER TIP TSWALU (123 E4) (*G4*)

The largest private nature reserve in southern Africa (covering 24.7 million acres) belongs to the Oppenheimer diamond family who have been honoured by the WWF for their conservation efforts. The lodge's suites are extremely luxurious. A big attraction is tracking rhino on foot. *(9 rooms | near to Kuruman | tel. 05 37 81 93 31 | www.tswalu.com | Expensive). 210km (130mi) from Kimberley*

KNYSNA

(127 E6) (*G8*) **Knysna (pop. 35,000) is a charming, colourful town and the unofficial capital of the Garden Route.** The town lies between a mountain range and a large lagoon that is connected to the sea by a narrow stretch of water. At the lagoon mouth are two sandstone cliffs, the *Knysna Heads,* one on each side of the lagoon. Knysna is a popular holiday destination for South Africans possibly because of the top class oysters farmed on the lagoon and of course there is also the famous *Knysna Forest*.

SIGHTSEEING

MILLWOOD HOUSE MUSEUM

Exhibits about the town's history and about the life of its founder, George Rex. *Lower Queen St | Mon–Fri 9.30am–4.30pm, Sat 9.30am–12.30pm | admission free*

FOOD & DRINK

INSIDER TIP FIREFLY EATING HOUSE
A mother and daughter team run this tiny curry restaurant, it only has five tables so reservations are essential. *152 a Old Cape Rd | tel. 04 43 82 14 90 | Budget*

ILE DE PAIN BREAD & CAFÉ
Serves heavenly breads and excellent breakfasts and lunches. *10 Boatshed | Thesens Island | tel. 04 43 02 57 07 | Budget*

ZACHARY'S
High up above the lagoon in the Pezula Resort Hotel and Spa is the best restaurant on the Garden Route, all dishes are made with organic produce. *Pezula Resort | tel. 04 43 02 33 33 | Expensive*

SHOPPING

FRENCH KISSES
Here you can buy colourful and authentic South African clothes by designers like Maya Prass, as well as unusual items from Europe and Asia. *Thesens Island*

THE WATERFRONT
All kinds of quaint shops can be found around the yacht harbour. Among these is the *Beach House* where you can buy the perfect sailing outfit. *Knysna Quays*

INSIDER TIP KNYSNA FINE ART
Sleepy Knysna happens to have one the country's best art galleries. Look out for the works of Hylton Nel. *6 Long St*

SPORTS & BEACHES

The *Elephant Walk* is a 21km (13mi) hiking trail that takes you through the Knysna Forest but the chance of spotting an elephant on the trail is slim. For golfers there is the *Knysna Golf Club (tel. 04 43 84 11 50)* and the *Pezula Golf Club (tel. 04 43 02 53 00)* in its spectacular setting. Water sport options are endless and if you are after something out of the ordinary then rent a houseboat for your overnight stay: *Lightley's Holiday Houseboats (tel. 04 43 86 00 07 | www.houseboats.co.za | Budget)*. Another option is *Knysna Charters (Thesens Island | tel. 08 28 92 04 69)*.

ENTERTAINMENT

34 DEGREES SOUTH
This restaurant and bar, with a view of the yacht harbour, comes alive during the holiday season. *Knysna Quays | Waterfront*

WHERE TO STAY

AFRICAN JEWEL LODGE
Backpackers get to stay in a stately Victorian house. The décor is colourful, typically African and there is a choice between a dormitory or having your own en suite room. *8 rooms | 2 Bond St | tel. 04 43 82 19 79 | www.africanjewel.co.za | Budget*

LOW BUDGET

▶ One of South Africa's most popular hiking trails is the *Otter Trail* on the Garden Route. It takes five days and you need to book it a year in advance. If you do not have a booking, you can still walk the first day of the hike that begins at the mouth of the Storms River and pay for it on site *(www.sanparks.org)*.

▶ A stop at the Billabong and Quiksilver *factory shops* in Jeffrey's Bay is an absolute must for the latest in surfing gear.

HOMTINI GUEST FARM

This is a working farm and guests are accommodated in cottages or in permanent tents. Spectacular mountain views and great hiking trails. *7 rooms | Homtini Pass | tel. 04 43 89 00 29 | www.homtini.co.za | Budget*

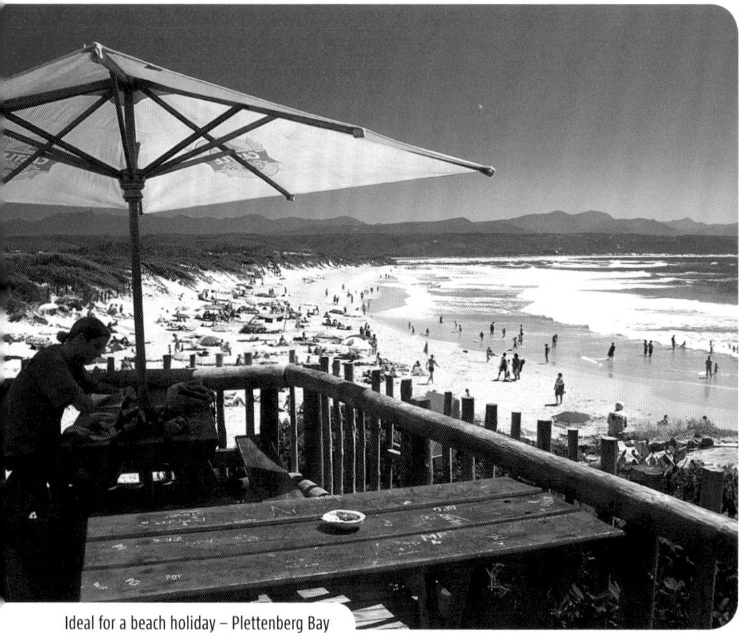

Ideal for a beach holiday – Plettenberg Bay

INSIDER TIP **TURBINE HOTEL**

A luxurious hotel in an old power station. The machinery and equipment are listed and the hotel has been built using environmentally friendly standards. *24 rooms | Thesens Island | tel. 04 43 02 57 46 | www.turbinehotel.co.za | Moderate*

INFORMATION

KNYSNA TOURISM

40 Main Rd | tel. 04 43 82 55 10 | www.visitknysna.com

WHERE TO GO

PLETTENBERG BAY

(127 E6) (G8)

In 1576 the Portuguese explorer Mesquita da Perestrelo gave this town 25km (15mi) from Knysna the name *Bahia Formosa*, meaning 'beautiful bay'. The town was later named after Joachim von Plettenberg who was governor in 1778. Today Plettenberg Bay is an exclusive holiday resort with three beautiful beaches stretching 7km (4.3mi). The beaches are ideal for children. On average the sun shines 320 days a year here and between July and September whales give birth to their young in the bay.

Right on the rocks at the water's edge is the luxury hotel *The Plettenberg* with unrivalled sea views. Its restaurant *Sand* is the best in town *(40 rooms | Look Out Rocks | tel. 04 45 33 20 23 | www.plettenberg.com | Expensive)*.

A few kilometres outside of town is INSIDER TIP *Emily Moon River Lodge*. Guests stay in eight spacious cottages with stunning views across the Bitou River *(8 rooms | Bitou Valley | tel. 04 45 33 29 82 | www.emilymoon.co.za | Moderate)*.

Above the famous Lookout Beach is the small *La Vista* guest house with its captivating views of the sea from the pool deck *(7 rooms | 17 Rosheen Crescent | tel. 04 45 33 30 08 | www.lavista.co.za | Moderate)*.

Restaurants in 'Plett' – short for Plettenberg Bay – that come highly recommended are the *Cornuti al Mare (1 Perestrella St | tel. 04 45 33 46 78 | Budget)* and the INSIDER TIP *Fu.Shi/Boma (3 Strand St | tel. 04 45 33 50 83 | Moderate)*.

Ocean Blue Adventures offers dolphin and whale viewing by boat trips. The company follows the strict guidelines set out by nature conservation *(tel. 04 45 33 50 83)*.

10km (6mi) outside of town you will come across South Africa's most beautiful tree house hotel, the *Tsala Treetop Lodge* – surrounded by ancient milkwood trees *(10 rooms | tel. 04 45 01 11 11 | www.hunterhotels.com/tsalatreetoplodge | Expensive)*

TSITSIKAMMA NATIONAL PARK

(127 F6) (*G8*)

This nature conservation area is made up of a 5km (3mi) coastal stretch that also extends 5km (3mi) into the ocean. To the interior is the Tsitsikamma Forest National Park which includes some virgin indigenous forest. There is also the impressive *Paul Sauer Bridge*. 192m (630ft) long it spans the Storms River at a height of 139m (456ft). The view from the bridge is breathtaking. For an overnight stay in these awesome surroundings, there is the *Tsitsikamma Village Inn (49 rooms | Storms River | tel. 04 22 81 17 11 | www.tsitsikammahotel.co.za | Moderate)*.

Adventure seekers may want stop in at *Stormsriver Adventure*. They offer water sports, horseback riding and mountain climbing *(tel. 04 22 81 18 36 | www.stormsriver.com)*.

LANGEBAAN

(126 B5) (*D7*) **This small sleepy town (population of 4600) lies right on the**

Suspension bridge over the Storms River

Langebaan lagoon which stretches over 16km (10mi) and is a true bird lover's paradise.
In the summer it is home to some 55,000 birds including herons, ibis, oystercatchers, greater and lesser flamingos and cormorants as well as other animals such as antelopes and zebras. Year round sunshine, calm waters and good winds make Langebaan a favourite resort destination for kite and windsurfers, fishermen and divers, particularly for its warm lagoon waters.

SIGHTSEEING

WEST COAST NATIONAL PARK ★

This small national park is a protected wetland habitat for endangered bird species. It encompasses the lagoon and a large part of the surrounding area and is regarded as one of South Africa's most significant wetlands.

FOOD & DRINK

INSIDER TIP STRANDLOPER

A rustic restaurant right on the beach that serves fish grilled on an open fire. *Beach | tel. 02 27 72 24 90 | Budget*

WHERE TO STAY

FARMHOUSE LANGEBAAN

This hotel forms part of an old farmhouse and has wonderful views of the lagoon and you will also be able to watch the flamingos from its terrace. *15 rooms | 5 Egret St | tel. 02 27 72 20 62 | www.thefarmhouse langebaan.co.za | Moderate*

INFORMATION

LANGEBAAN TOURISM BUREAU

Corner Bree St and Hoof St | tel. 02 27 72 15 15 | www.langebaaninfo.co.za

WHERE TO GO

PATERNOSTER

(126 B5) *(D7)*
A romantic fishing village with whitewashed cottages. Stay at the *Blue Dolphin B & B (4 rooms | 12 Warrel Klip St | tel. 02 27 52 20 01 | www.bluedolphin.co.za | Budget)* right by the sea and treat yourself to some of the best west coast seafood at the *Noisy Oyster (tel. 02 27 52 2196 | Budget). 40km (25mi) north-west of Langebaan*

PORT ELIZABETH

(128 A6) *(H8)* **This harbour city (population of 1.5 million) was named after the wife of its founder, Sir Rufane Donkin. South Africans simply call it 'PE'.**
Even though the British built a fort here in 1799, it was only settled two decades later in 1820. Today PE is the centre of the country's motor vehicle industry: Ford, Opel and Volkswagen are all manufactured here. Despite it being a commercial hub the city has been able to retain its Victorian charm and is a sought-after holiday destination. It stretches 16km (10mi)

CITY WHERE TO START?
The **Market Square** is the historical part of PE which has some noteworthy buildings like the city hall. From here head west to Donkin Street with its well preserved Victorian houses. The **Tourist Information** is in the Donkin Lighthouse Building where the 5km (3mi) Donkin Trail begins. Try Chapel Street and Victoria Street for parking.

along Algoa Bay with its magnificent sandy beaches.

SIGHTSEEING

BAYWORLD MUSEUM COMPLEX

The museum has an exhibition detailing the city's history as well as a section about the indigenous Xhosa tribes. Next door is the *Oceanarium* and *Aquarium*. *Beach Rd | daily 9am–4.30pm | entrance fee 35 rand*

CAMPANILE

Built in 1923 this 53m(173ft) tower is a memorial to commemorate the first landing of the British in Port Elizabeth and has an excellent view of the city. Its 23 bells chime at 8.22am, 1.32pm and 6.02pm. *Strand St | Tue–Sat 9am–12.30pm and 1.30–5pm, Sun/Mon 2–5pm*

NO. 7 CASTLE HILL MUSEUM

Museum complex with settler's house dating back to 1827. *7 Castle Hill St | Mon–Thu 9am–1pm and 2–4pm | entrance fee 20 rand*

ST GEORGES PARK

This expansive park in the city centre is home to the Botanical Garden and the *Nelson Mandela Metropolitan Art Museum*, a showcase for Eastern Cape artists.

Port Elizabeth's spacious Market Square and city hall

FOOD & DRINK

INSIDER TIP CUBATA

Next to the new World Cup stadium, this cosy restaurant specialises in Portuguese dishes. Reservations essential! *Arthur Rd | tel. 08 36 72 66 83 |* Budget

March of the elephants – Addo Elephant National Park

34° SOUTH
Restaurant with a view, on the Boardwalk complex. Recommended are its seafood starters. *The Boardwalk Casino and Entertainment World | Marine Drive | tel. 04 15 83 10 85 |* Moderate

SHOPPING

INSIDER TIP **MELVILLE & MOON**
A great store for all the safari gear you will need for that mandatory excursion to one of the Eastern Cape's game parks. *The Gasworks | Korsten St*

SPORTS & ACTIVITIES

Surfing gear can be hired on just about every beach and you can also scuba dive in the ship wrecks off the coast *(Pro Dive | tel. 04 15 81 11 44)*. Sand boarding is also becoming increasingly popular *(information tel. 04 15 83 20 23)*.

ENTERTAINMENT

CUBANA
Ultra-modern bar with sea and harbour views. *Kings Beach*

ESCOBAR
Dance the night away! *Moffet on Main Lifestyle Centre, Walmer*

WHERE TO STAY

THE BEACH HOTEL
A stylish hotel right on the famous *Hobie Beach* with stunning breakfast terrace. *58 rooms | Marine Drive | tel. 04 15 83 21 61 | www.pehotels.co.za |* Moderate

INSIDER TIP **SHAMWARI TOWNHOUSE**
Chic hotel with art deco furnishings and an exquisite art collection. *7 rooms | 8 Brighton Dr | tel. 04 15 02 60 00 | www.shamwaritownhouse.com |* Expensive

INFORMATION

TOURIST INFORMATION
Donkin Lighthouse Building | tel. 04 15 82 25 75 | www.nmbt.co.za

WHERE TO GO

ADDO ELEPHANT NATIONAL PARK ★ (128 A6) (*H7–8*)
More than 400 elephants in more than 400,000 acres of national park, 60km (37mi) from Port Elizabeth. When the reserve was opened in 1931 it had only eleven elephants. Today it is also home to the Big Five (buffalo, elephant, lion, leopard and rhino) and the park has expanded into the sea and now also includes southern right whales and great white sharks i.e the Big Seven. *7am–7pm daily | entrance fee 130 rand per person* 5km (3mi) from the main entrance is the *Addo Dung Beetle Guest Farm (5 rooms | tel. 08 39 74 58 02 | www.woodall-addo.co.za | Moderate).*

GRAHAMSTOWN (128 B5) (*H7*)
During the winter holidays this small university town transforms itself into a festival venue that draws visitors from all over the world. There are theatre and opera performances, a dynamic line-up of fringe events and street festivals *(details from Tourist Information | tel. 04 66 22 32 41).* The first settlers arrived here in 1820 and today visitors can stay in two of their original houses *(Settlers Hill Cottages | 10 rooms | 42 Market St | tel. 04 66 22 42 43 | www.settlershill-cottages.co.za | Budget).* If you had something more luxurious in mind then look no further than *7 Worcester Street (10 rooms. | 7 Worcester St | tel. 04 66 22 28 43 | www.worcesterstreet.co.za | Moderate). 110km (68mi) north-east of Port Elizabeth*

JEFFREY'S BAY ● (128 A6) (*H8*)
This small coastal resort 75km (46mi) west of Port Elizabeth has the best waves in South Africa and its superb beach is great even for those who don't surf. The *Beach House (4 rooms | 18 Pepper St | tel. 04 22 93 15 22 | www.jbaybeachhouse.co.za | Budget)* lies right on the beach. Make sure you book a corner room on the first floor INSIDER TIP for a sea view. For surfing lessons speak to Etienne Venter at *Jeffrey's Bay Surfing School (tel. 04 22 93 42 14).* Bargain hunting at the *Billabong* and *Quicksilver* factory shops is an absolute must. *160km (100mi) from Port Elizabeth*

DIAMOND DIVING

It is not a widely known fact that diamonds are found not only in mines but also in the seabed. The Atlantic Ocean between Langebaan and the Namibian border is divided into grids for which companies buy diving rights. Divers dive down to the seabed from boats with vacuuming equipment and then the diamond-bearing sand and stone is drawn to the surface through flexible hoses. Diamonds found among the course gravel have to be handed in at a state-controlled inspection point. The price is controlled and theft is a highly punishable offence. Most of these adventure seeking divers live in the rather barren coastal town of Port Nolloth.

CAPE TOWN & SURROUNDS

Cape Town is an urban delight: exclusive suburbs, a lively harbour area and a peninsula that boasts quaint fishing villages, scenic coastal roads, superb beaches, nature reserves and Cape Point.

The peninsula south of Cape Town is 51km (31mi) long and at no point wider than 16km (10mi). The suburb of Constantia was where the Cape wine industry first started some 300 years ago and the surrounding farms have joined up for their own popular wine route. The small village of Franschhoek was settled by French Huguenots who planted the first vines and established a community that would go on to become the country's culinary capital. The university town of Stellenbosch has not only one of the country's best universities but is also home to some excellent wine farms. Nearby Paarl is where Nelson Mandela spent his final prison years and it was from here that he walked through the prison gate to freedom on one of the exceptionally hot days that Paarl is famous for.

For Capetonians Hermanus is a favourite weekend and summer holiday getaway, the further up the east coast you travel the warmer the Atlantic currents are (often 20° C/68° F in the summer) and its long stretches of beach are excellent for hikes.

Photo: Camps Bay beach

Superb city with stunning environs where beautiful bays, lush wine lands and huge mountain ranges all lie closely together

CAPE TOWN

MAP INSIDE BACK COVER
(126 B5–6) (*D8*) **Both seasoned travellers and locals are of the opinion that Cape Town (population of 3.3 million) is the world's most beautiful city.** You get the best view of Cape Town when you arrive by ship. The sight of the city extending up the slopes of the mountain is awe-inspiring as is Table Mountain itself, draped by a 'tablecloth' of clouds on most mornings from December to April. In the bay beneath the mountain lies the harbour. The rocky seabed meant that it had to be built far out to sea in order to attain the depths needed. The oldest section surrounding the Victoria and Alfred basins have now been converted in to the popu-

In the Gold of Africa Museum

lar V & A Waterfront entertainment area with restaurants, shops, museums and theatres.

Cape Town's economy is based on its tourism and its commercial harbour. Spoilt by their magnificent surroundings Capetonians are cheerful, easy going and know how to make the most of their city. Their laissez faire approach to life means that they seldom get worked up or stressed out, an attitude jokingly known as the 'Cape coma'.

At the tip of the peninsula is the Cape of Good Hope and this is where the Atlantic and Indian Oceans meet. The water along the coast warms up as you travel further east, one of the reasons why Hermanus is such a popular destination. The town is also renowned as the world's best land-based whale watching location. Between June and December the females give birth in the bay. Further up the coast, near to Bredasdrop is Africa's most southerly tip, Cape Agulhas and this is also where migratory white storks spend the European winter.

The MARCO POLO Cape Town travel guide will have more in-depth information.

> **CITY WHERE TO START?**
> The ideal starting point to set out from is **Green Market Square**. From here head past the old city hall to **St Georges Cathedral**, behind the church is where the *Company's Garden* begins. Find parking in Loop or Long Street or in the Christian Barnard Memorial Hospital car park between Buitengracht and Bree Street.

SIGHTSEEING

BO KAAP (MALAY QUARTER)

(U B3) (*b3*)

A century and a half ago the colourful houses of this suburb were home to slaves from Malaysia. After the end of apartheid the quarter became a melting pot of cultures and religions.

CASTLE OF GOOD HOPE ●

(U C5–6) (*c5–6*)

Fortified with canons this fortress, South Africa's oldest building, was built in 1666 as the residence of the first governor of the Cape and to protect the settlers. Housed inside its pentagonal ramparts is an Africana collection and military museum. *Castle St | Mon–Sat 10am–4pm | guided tours 10am, 11am, noon and 2pm | Dec–Jan every 30 minutes | entrance fee 25 rand*

DISTRICT SIX MUSEUM
(U B5) *(🗺 b5)*
Photo exhibition covering the forced evictions of its residents by the apartheid government. *25A Buitenkant St | Mon–Sat 9am–4pm | entrance fee 15 rand*

INSIDER TIP **GOLD OF AFRICA MUSEUM**
(U C3) *(🗺 c3)*
The Anglo Gold Ashanti group bought the historical Martin Melck House in 2001 to display their important collection of West African gold art and ancient jewellery from southern Africa. Its *Gold* restaurant serves dishes from around Africa *(Moderate). 96 Strand St | Mon–Sat 9.30am–5pm | entrance fee 20 rand*

GROOT CONSTANTIA ● (0) *(🗺 0)*
This is the oldest wine estate in Africa and the manor house is a particularly impressive example of Cape Dutch architecture. Wine tasting available and two restaurants on site with outdoor seating options. Light contemporary cuisine is served at *Simon's (tel. 02 17 94 11 43 | Moderate). Groot Constantia Rd | 9am–5pm*

JEWISH MUSEUM (U A5) *(🗺 a5)*
An exhibition about the past 150 years of Jewish history in South Africa, while the *Holocaust Centre* next door portrays the fate of Jews who had fled to South Africa from Nazi Europe. *88 Hatfield St | Sun–Thu 10am–5pm, Fri 10am–2pm | entrance fee 35 rand*

KIRSTENBOSCH BOTANICAL GARDENS ★ (0) *(🗺 0)*
On the eastern slopes of Table Mountain at a height of 100m (328ft) to 1000m (3280ft) are the famed botanical gardens, home to just about every South African floral and tree species. August to October is the best time to admire the remarkable displays of spring blossoms. There is a large glass conservatory and a good restaurant *(Budget). M 3 in the direction of Constantia then turn right into Rhodes Drive | daily Sept–March 8am–7pm, April–Aug 8am–6pm | entrance fee 32 rand*

INSIDER TIP **LONG STREET BATHS** ●
(U A3) *(🗺 a3)*
Dating back to 1908 this modernised and heated indoor swimming pool is 25m

MARCO POLO HIGHLIGHTS

★ Kirstenbosch Botanical Gardens
The best time to visit is during the South African spring which is from August to October → p. 51

★ Table Mountain
The fit and adventurous can hike up to the 1000m (3280ft) summit but there is always the cable car option → p. 53

★ Cape Agulhas
Confluence of the warm Indian Ocean and cold Atlantic → p. 58

★ Cape of Good Hope
Magnificent lookout point on the tip of Cape Point with expansive views over the peninsula and the ocean → p. 57

★ KWV
In Paarl join a fascinating tour of the wine cellars of the country's largest wine producer → p. 62

★ Stellenbosch
A delightful and historic town (one of South Africa's oldest) right in the middle of the wine producing area → p. 64

(82ft) and also offers the option for you to indulge in a Turkish bath. *Corner Long St/Orange St | 7am–7pm daily | entrance fee 12 rand*

PARLIAMENT AND TUYNHUIS
(U A–B4) (🕮 a–b4)

Along the south side of Government Avenue is the back of the Houses of Parliament. When parliament is in progress the buildings can only be viewed with prior bookings. Alongside it, in the Company's Garden, is *Tuynhuis* the presidential seat since 1751. *Tours tel. 02148 76800 | admission free (don't forget your passport!)*

ROBBEN ISLAND MUSEUM (O) (🕮 O)

Tours of the island, where Nelson Mandela and other political prisoners were once held, take three hours and are best booked in advance *(departures 9am, 11am, 1pm and 3pm daily). Clocktower Terminal | Waterfront | tel. 0214194263 | rimbookings @robben-island.org.za | ticket 180 rand*

ST GEORGE'S CATHEDRAL
(U B4) (🕮 b4)

Victorian cathedral and seat of the Anglican archbishop. This was also where Nobel Peace Prize laureate Desmond Tutu gave his sermons which were critical of the apartheid government of the time. *Corner Queen Victoria St/Wale St | Mon–Fri 6.30am–5.30pm, Sat/Sun 6.30am–1pm*

SOUTH AFRICAN NATIONAL GALLERY
(U A4–5) (🕮 a4–5)

South Africa's most significant art museum showcasing African and European art. *Government Ave | Tue–Sun 10am–5pm | entrance fee 15 rand*

Houses of Parliament and Tuynhuis in Cape Town

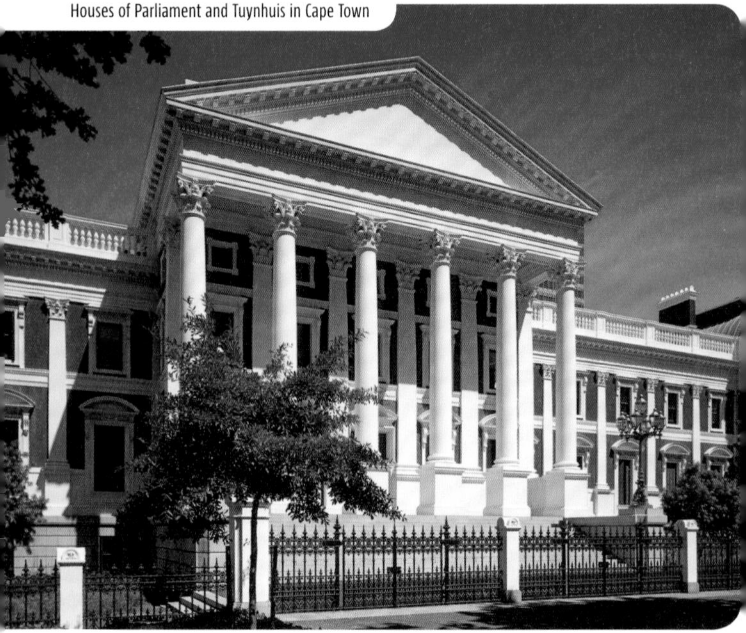

TABLE MOUNTAIN ★ ☆
(0) (*m 0*)

No visit to Cape Town is complete without the mandatory trip up Table Mountain. It takes the cable car only five minutes to reach the summit 1086m (3562ft) above the city. There are also a number of hiking paths like the ● *Platteklip Gorge* route. The cable car runs all year round weather permitting (price approx. 145 rand). The *Sundowner Special* after 6pm in summer is INSIDERTIP half price and is the perfect opportunity to watch the sun set over the Atlantic. *Tafelberg Rd | cable car May–Nov 8.30am–5pm, Nov–April 8am–9pm | weather information tel. 02 14 24 81 81*

VICTORIA & ALFRED WATERFRONT ●
(U F1–2) (*m f1–2*)

The oldest section of the harbour was named after Queen Victoria and her second son Alfred who laid its foundation stone in 1860. Today it is simply referred to as the *V & A Waterfront* and is an unrivalled entertainment precinct with museums, hotels, an amphitheatre, restaurants, cinemas and international and local designer stores. Visit the acclaimed *Two Oceans Aquarium (9.30am–6pm daily | entrance fee 100 rand)*. *Waterfront Visitors Centre | tel. 02 14 08 76 00 | www.waterfront.co.za*

FOOD & DRINK

AUBERGINE
(U A6) (*m a6*)

Sophisticated and elegant dining is the order of the day in this award-winning restaurant. *39 Barnet St | tel. 2 14 65 49 09 | Expensive*

BIZERCA
(U D4) (*m d4*)

Great restaurant that is ideal for a city lunch. *15 Anton Anreith Arcade/Jetty St | tel. 21 41 88 00 11 | Budget*

BUITENVERWACHTING ☆ (0) (*m 0*)

A fine dining restaurant set amidst vineyards in the suburb of Constantia. Their wines are also excellent. *Klein Constantia Rd | tel. 02 17 94 35 22 | Expensive*

INSIDERTIP CARNE (U A4) (*m a4*)

Reserve a table well in advance so not to miss out on the city's best steaks. *70 Keroom St | tel. 02 14 24 34 60 | Moderate*

INSIDERTIP FOODBARN RESTAURANT
☺ (0) (*m 0*)

Owner and top chef Franck Dangereux worked in a number of fine restaurants before opening his own in rural Noordhoek. His ingredients are all organic and his dishes are always delicious. *Farm Village Lane | tel. 02 17 89 13 90 | Budget*

GRAND BEACH ● (0) (*m 0*)

Cape Town's only restaurant on the beach is in Granger Bay next to the Waterfront and is the perfect spot to enjoy your sundowners with your feet in the sand. *Beach Rd | tel. 02 14 25 05 51 | Moderate*

MARCO'S AFRICA PLACE
(U C3) (*m c3*)

The best of Africa's culinary fare is served in this popular restaurant. *15 Rose Lane, Bo Kaap | tel. 02 14 23 54 12 | Budget*

MARIO'S (0) (*m 0*)

Going strong for over 30 years, this is one of Cape Town's best Italian restaurants. *89 Main Rd | tel. 02 14 39 66 44 | Budget*

OBZ CAFÉ (0) (*m 0*)

Very popular with students – live music on weekends. *115 Lower Main Rd | Observatory*

THE ROUNDHOUSE ☆ (0) (*m 0*)

Top restaurant in an historic building, on the mountain above Camps Bay. *Kloof Rd | tel. 02 14 38 43 47 | Expensive*

Stop for a bite to eat after your Church Street shopping spree

SHOPPING

CAPE COBRA (U F1) (*f1*)
Your best bet for good quality ostrich leather items like handbags and belts. *4th Floor, Hill House | 43 Somerset Rd*

CHURCH STREET (U B4) (*b4*)
Between Long Street and Burg Street is the Church Street pedestrian zone with its selection of shops, galleries, antique stores, restaurants and street cafés. Also worth a visit is the *AVA Gallery* a non-profit organisation that promotes talented young artists. *35 Church St*

INSIDER TIP **CHRISTOFF**
(U F1) (*f1*)
In the *V & A Waterfront*, this is one of Cape Town's best jewellers – the semi-precious stone creations are particularly popular. *Shop 7217*

EVERARD READ GALLERY
(U E1) (*e1*)
Reputable gallery with a wide selection of the country's best contemporary artists. *3 Portswood Rd*

INSIDER TIP **MONKEY BIZ**
(U B3) (*b3*)
A craft project that offers employment opportunities to disadvantaged women. The women sell their exceptional beaded objects and art. *43 Rose St*

VAUGHAN JOHNSON'S WINE SHOP
(U F1) (*f1*)
Connoisseur Vaughan Johnson will be at your service to advise you. Excellent selec-

tion of wines on offer. *V&A Waterfront | www.vaughanjohnson.com*

SPORTS & ACTIVITIES

You can hire a yacht from the *Waterfront Boat Company* in the harbour *(tel. 02 14 18 58 06)* or if golf is more your style then you will have a good selection of clubs like the *Royal Cape Golf Club | tel. 02 17 61 65 51*. And if you prefer something a little less active then Clifton's four wind-protected beaches are Cape Town's finest. The ● *One & Only Hotel* in Dock Road offers its guests spa treatments inspired by Africa's own natural environment.

ENTERTAINMENT

In the evening most of the action takes place at the *V&A Waterfront* (U F1–2) *(🕮 f1–2)* or in the city centre around *Long Street* and *Kloof Street* (U A4) (*🕮* a4). Also worth a mention:

INSIDER TIP BANG BANG CLUB
(U B4) *(🕮 b4)*

One of the most popular clubs in Cape Town with hip local and international music. *70 Long St | entrance fee 30 rand*

PLANET BAR (O) *(🕮 O)*

The stylish and funky décor of the colonial Mount Nelson hotel's bar makes it a must. *76 Orange St*

TRINITY (U D2) *(🕮 d2)*

This entertainment Mecca boasts numerous restaurants and is Cape Town's only super club. *15 Bennet St*

WHERE TO STAY

AFRICAN TRAIN LODGE (U D5) *(🕮 d5)*

A fun and affordable accommodation option that is centrally located behind the station. Spend the night in an old railway carriage and have breakfast in the dining car. *60 rooms | Old Marine Drive | tel. 02 14 18 48 90 | www.trainlodge.co.za | Budget*

THE BACKPACK
(O) *(🕮 O)*

An old favourite, this backpacker hotel is also centrally located. You must try their signature 'safari' breakfast. *30 rooms | 74 New Church St | tel. 02 14 34 45 30 | www.backpackers.co.za | Budget*

INSIDER TIP FIRE AND ICE
(U B3) *(🕮 b3)*

Ultra hip hotel with pool, aquarium, climbing wall and a collection of surfboards. *105 rooms | New Church St/Victoria St | tel. 02 14 88 25 55 | www.proteahotels.com | Budget*

GRAND DADDY
(U C4) *(🕮 c4)*

This chic hotel with a super bar and excellent restaurant is right in the middle of the city. If you stay here you can even spend the night in an American INSIDER TIP *Airstream Trailer* on their penthouse 'trailer park'. *25 rooms | 38 Long St | tel. 02 14 24 72 47 | www.granddaddy.co.za | Moderate*

HOUT BAY MANOR
(O) *(🕮 O)*

A Victorian hotel that has been revitalised with a colourful African touch. *21 rooms | Baviaanskloof, off Main Rd | tel. 02 17 90 01 16 | www.houtbaymanor.com | Expensive*

KOPANONG B & B
(O) *(🕮 O)*

A tiny township guest house in Khayelitsha. The owner also offers her guests tours of the community. *3 rooms | C 329 Velani Crescent | tel. 02 13 61 20 84 | www.kopanong-township.co.za | Budget*

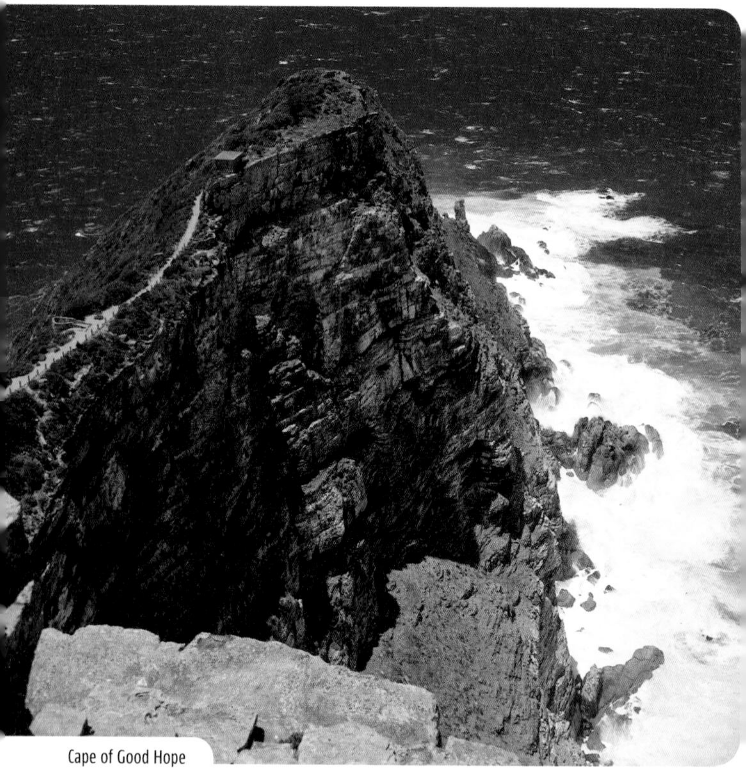

Cape of Good Hope

STEENBERG HOTEL (O) (🕮 O)
Only 20 minutes from the city centre, this elegant hotel is surrounded by a golf course and vineyards. *16 rooms | Tokai Rd | Constantia | tel. 02 17 13 22 22 | www.steenberg.com* | *Expensive*

THE VINEYARD HOTEL AND SPA ●
(O) (🕮 O)
This hotel and spa in a park at the foot of Table Mountain has to be Cape Town's INSIDER TIP most magnificent wellness oasis, the hotel belongs to the renowned *Banyan Tree Group. 173 rooms | Coliton Rd | Newlands | tel. 02 16 57 45 00 | www.vineyard.co.za* | *Moderate*

WINCHESTER MANSION
(O) (🕮 O)
Very traditional hotel located on the Sea Point promenade. *76 rooms | 221 Beach Rd | tel. 02 14 34 23 51 | www.winchester.co.za* | *Moderate*

INFORMATION

CAPE TOWN TOURISM (U C4) (🕮 c4)
Corner Burg St/Castle St | tel. 02 14 26 42 60 | www.tourismcapetown.com

TOURISM CENTRE WATERFRONT
(U E2) (🕮 e2)
Clock Tower Precinct | tel. 02 14 05 45 00

WHERE TO GO

CHAPMAN'S PEAK DRIVE
(126 B6) (*D8*)

The route from *Hout Bay* to the Cape of Good Hope is via this spectacular coastal drive. In the 1920s the road was hewn from the mountain rock face. The 10km (6.2mi) drive cuts through overhanging rocky outcrops and its 133 bends wind high above the lashing ocean. It is well worth every cent of the 30 rand toll fee per car. *15km (9.3mi) from Cape Town*

CAPE OF GOOD HOPE ★
(126 B6) (*D8*)

The Cape of Good Hope is at the southernmost tip of the peninsula and forms part of a nature reserve. It is often erroneously believed to be the tip of Africa. When Bartholomew Diaz first sailed around the Cape he called it the Cape of Storms. True to its name the weather can be volatile here so check the weather report before you take the drive. Once there, a funicular takes you up 40m (131ft) to the top of *Cape Point* then you have 133 steps to climb to reach the lighthouse. The vantage point gives you a breathtaking view of the sea and the peninsula. *6am–6pm daily | entrance fee 80 rand per person and 45 rand for the funicular | 60km (37mi) from Cape Town*

SIMON'S TOWN
(126 B6) (*D8*)

Located some 20km (12.4mi) south of Cape Town it has been a naval base for the past 300 years. Stop for a seafood lunch at the *Black Marlin* and watch the whales from your table *(Millers Point | tel. 02 17 86 16 21 | Moderate)*.

The coastal stretch a few kilometres further south is of particular interest for its penguin colony. There is a viewing platform where you can watch their antics or INSIDER TIP you can swim with them at the neighbouring beach *(Boulders Beach | entrance fee 35 rand | 50km (31mi) from Cape Town)*.

Penguins at Boulders Beach south of Simon's Town

BREDASDORP

(126 C6) (🕮 E8) **The town (population of 10,000) was established in 1838 by Michiel van Breda and today it is the administrative centre of the region.**
The area is very popular with visitors who come for the biodiversity of the natural vegetation, the *fynbos*. This small area is home to a remarkable 6000 of the 8000 species of *fynbos*. It is also an ideal spot for bird watching

SIGHTSEEING

HEUNINGBERG NATURE RESERVE

Bredasdorp's botanical reserve is also home to an abundance of *fynbos* species, some endemic. *Van Riebeck St | 9am–6pm daily | entrance fee 15 rand*

SHIPWRECK MUSEUM

Cape Agulhas is well known as the 'ships' graveyard' and the museum displays the treasures retrieved from some of the 125 ships that have gone down here since the 16th century. *6 Independent St | Mon–Fri 9am–3pm, Sat/Sun 11am–3.45pm | entrance fee 10 rand*

FOOD & DRINK

JULIANS

Owner Julian has opened a restaurant next to his pottery studio and the crockery is all designed by artist himself. *22 All Saints St | tel. 02 84 25 12 01 | Moderate*

SHOPPING

INSIDER TIP KAPULA GALLERY

The gallery produces elaborate and colourful candles with ethnic designs that are exported worldwide. *Corner Patterson Rd/ First Ave*

WHERE TO STAY

FIRLANE HOUSE

Colonial charm awaits guests to this small eight-roomed guest house in the centre of town. *5 Firlane Rd | tel. 02 84 25 28 08 | www.firlanehouse.co.za | Moderate*

INFORMATION

CAPE AGULHAS TOURISM OFFICE

Dr. Jansen St | tel. 02 84 24 25 84 | www.tourismcapeagulhas.co.za

WHERE TO GO

CAPE AGULHAS ★

(126 C6) (🕮 E8)

This is Africa's southernmost tip and even if it seems isolated and unspectacular, the sensation of having the whole of Africa behind you will certainly leave a lasting impression. The lighthouse dates back to 1848 and is open to visitors *(9am–5pm daily | entrance fee 15 rand)*. The *Agulhas Lighthouse Restaurant | Moderate*, serves meals and teas all day. Stay over at the *Agulhas Country Lodge (8 rooms | Main Rd | tel. 02 84 35 76 50 | www.agulhascountrylodge.com | Moderate)*. Their restaurant also has an excellent reputation. *39km (24mi) from Bredasdorp*

FRANSCH-HOEK

(126 B5) (🕮 D8) **This small town (population of 13,000) is nestled in a magnificent valley in the heart of the wine growing region. It was founded in 1688 by 152 Huguenots who fled religious persecution in France.**
Many of them came from wine producing regions and realised that the climate in

Franschhoek made it ideal for grapevines. The wine estates in and around Franschhoek all belong to the *Vignerons de Franschhoek* and almost all offer wine tastings.

SIGHTSEEING

INSIDER TIP FRANSCHHOEK MOTOR MUSEUM ●

A unique collection of more than 200 vintage cars on the L'Ormarins wine estate. *Tue–Fri 10am–4pm, Sat/Sun 10am–3pm | entrance fee 60 rand*

FRANSCHHOEK PASS ●

It is worth taking a drive up the awe-inspiring mountain pass that starts just as you leave Franschhoek. The first settlers called it Elephant Pass because herds of elephants used it as a route into the valley. Today you get a fantastic view of the vineyards and orchards from the top of the pass.

HUGUENOT MEMORIAL MUSEUM

Exhibits illustrating the history of the Huguenot settlers and the village. *Lambrecht St | Mon–Sat 9am–5pm, Sun 2pm–5pm | entrance fee 10 rand*

FOOD & DRINK

LE BON VIVANT

Excellent food at reasonable prices. The soups and trout dishes come highly recommended. *22 Dirkie Uys St | tel. 02 18 76 27 17 | Budget*

HAUTE CABRIÈRE

Your hosts Hildegard and Achim von Arnim have opened a stunning restaurant above

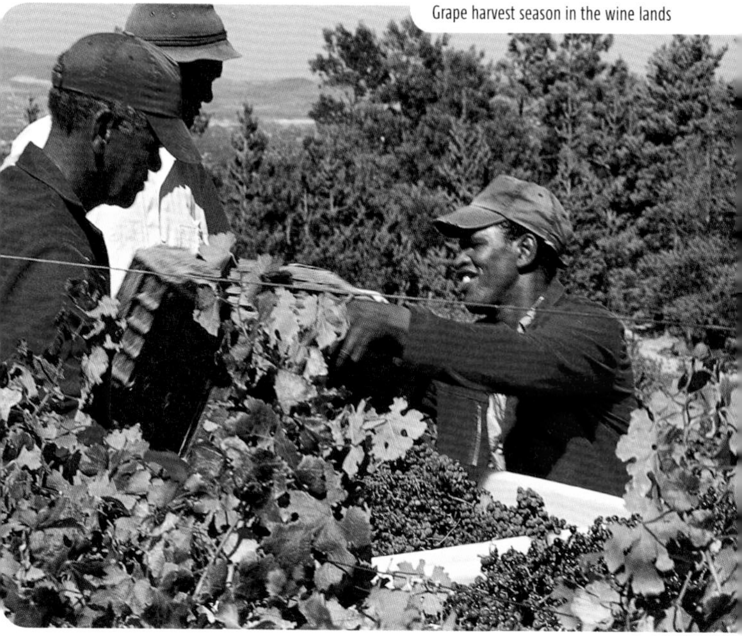

Grape harvest season in the wine lands

their wine cellar built into the mountain. *Pass Rd | tel. 02 18 76 36 88 | www.cabriere.co.za* | Moderate

Boschendal's Cape Dutch manor house

TASTING ROOM AT LE QUARTIER FRANÇAIS

This restaurant in the *Relais & Chateaux Hôtel* is regularly voted one of the best in the world. For some memorable fine dining try their eight-course set menu. *16 Huguenot Rd | tel. 02 18 76 21 51* | Moderate

INSIDER TIP REUBEN'S

Chef Reuben Riffel is one of South Africa's top chefs. Here's your opportunity to see for yourself what this young chef can produce. *Oude Stallen Centre | 19 Huguenot Rd | tel. 02 18 76 37 72 | www. reubens.co.za* | Budget

SHOPPING

INSIDER TIP DAVID WALTERS CERAMIC GALLERY

Roubaix House is the home, studio and gallery of this well known ceramicist. *24 Dirkie Uys St*

TSONGA GALLERY

Huge selection of fine and decorative arts from all over Africa. *40 Huguenot St | tel. 02 83 13 21 37* | Budget

WHERE TO STAY

AUBERGE CLERMONT

Surrounded by vineyards the estate's old wine cellar has been converted into guest rooms. *6 rooms | Robertsvlei Rd | tel. 02 18 76 37 00 | www.clermont.co.za* | Moderate

DIEU DONNE GUEST FARM

This small guest house some 4km (2½mi) from town is a peaceful oasis. *8 rooms | access from the R 45 | tel. 02 18 76 21 31 | www.dieudonne.co.za* | Budget

INSIDER TIP LA RESIDENCE

Ultra luxurious hotel set in the mountains above Franschhoek. *11 rooms | Elandskloof Private Rd | tel. 02 18 76 41 00 | www. laresidence.co.za* | Expensive

INFORMATION

FRANSCHHOEK WINE VALLEY AND TOURISM ASSOCIATION
70 Huguenot Rd | tel. 02 18 76 36 03 | www.franschhoek.org.za

WHERE TO GO

BOSCHENDAL
(126 B5) (*🕮 D8*)
This estate in the Drakenstein Valley is one of South Africa's most magnificent and it also has a restaurant and wine bar where you can taste some of their world famous wines *(wine tasting Mon–Sat 8.30am–4.30pm, Sun 9am–12.30pm | tel. 02 18 70 42 74 | Budget)*. In summer they have picnics under the beautiful oak trees. *15km (9.3mi) from Franschhoek*

HERMANUS

(126 C6) (*🕮 D8*) **Nestled between the ocean and mountains this town (population of 25, 000) was established by farmers in the 19th century.**
It did not take long for the tourists to arrive, drawn by the temperate climate and expansive beaches. During peak season from December to January it is almost impossible to find accommodation. Try to come out of season as this village is a jewel and worth a visit. From June to November the *southern right whales* make their appearance close to the coast – one of the best spots in the world for whale watching from the land and completely ● free of charge.

SIGHTSEEING

OLD HARBOUR MUSEUM
An informative exhibition with items used in the local fishing industry. Also information about whales and you can listen to the pre-recorded sounds of whales and other sea creatures. *Old Harbour | Mon–Sat 9am–5pm, Sun noon–4pm | entrance fee 5 rand*

FOOD & DRINK

INSIDER TIP **BIENTANG'S CAVE**
Built into the rocks right above the sea, this is one of the most unique restaurant settings in the world and you get to watch the whales while you eat. *Below Marine Dr | tel. 02 83 12 34 54 | Budget*

DELI
A small bistro serving daily specials and snacks. *181 Main Rd | tel. 02 83 13 21 37 | Budget*

HARBOUR ROCK
Enjoy fresh seafood and a superb view of Walker Bay. *Site 24A, New Harbour | tel. 02 83 12 29 20 | Moderate*

LOW BUDGET

▶ A romantic and affordable alternative to eating out is dinner on the beach. In Hout Bay you can buy fresh fish at the harbour in the morning and have a *braai* on the beach in the evening. And you will still have plenty of room in your budget for a 'Superquaffer of the Year' bottle of wine from John Platter's guide.

▶ For hotel comfort at backpacker prices opt for Daddy Long Legs on trendy Long Street. *13 rooms | 134 Long St | tel. 02 14 22 30 74 | www.daddylonglegs.co.za | Budget*

SPORTS & ACTIVITIES

Shark-cage diving is a real adventure and now is your opportunity to get up close and personal with a great white. *Great White Shark Diving | tel. 02 83 12 42 93 | www.greatwhitesharkdiving.com*

WHERE TO STAY

BIRKENHEAD HOUSE

This hotel is in the best location high up on the cliffs above the bay with amazing views out to sea and access to a lovely beach. *11 rooms | 119 7th Ave | tel. 02 83 14 80 00 | www.birkenheadhouse.com | Expensive*

WINDSOR HOTEL

Also on the cliffs above the steep coast, this hotel is full of old world charm. Stunning views. *60 rooms | 49 Marine Drive | tel. 02 83 12 37 27 | www.windsorhotel.co.za | Budget*

INFORMATION

HERMANUS TOURISM BUREAU

Old Station Building | Mitchell St | tel. 02 83 12 26 29 | www.hermanus.co.za

WHERE TO GO

KLEINBAAI (126 C6) (*D8*)

A fishing village some 30km (18mi) north of Hermanus. For plenty of rest, a great view and top-notch service stay at *Aire Del Mar (5 rooms | 77 Van Dyk St | tel. 02 83 84 28 48 | Budget)* right in the middle of the dunes.

For boat excursions out to the whales between June and November, the INSIDER TIP *Whale Whisperer (tel. 02 83 84 04 06 | www.whalewatchsa.com | ticket 900 rand)* comes highly recommended. The company is also involved in whale research.

PAARL

(126 B5) (*D8*) **Established in 1717 Paarl (population of 75,000) is the largest town in the wine lands.**

Its name derives from the massive granite rock above the town that shimmers like a pearl when the sun catches it. It was here in 1875 that the world's youngest language – Afrikaans – was declared an official language. The monument that pays tribute to this can be seen from miles away. It was from Paarl's *Victor Verster*, now called *Groot Drakenstein Prison*, that Nelson Mandela was released in 1990.

SIGHTSEEING

KWV ★

By far the world's largest wine and brandy cellar. *Kohler St | tours 10am, 10.30am and 2.15pm daily | tel. 02 18 07 30 08 | entrance fee 30 rand*

PAARL MUSEUM

An interesting exhibit that covers the architectural aspects of the town that also includes an impressive collection of Cape Dutch furniture. *303 Main St | Mon–Fri 10am–5pm, Sat 9am–3pm | entrance 10 rand*

FOOD & DRINK

MARC'S

Option of being outside under the lemon trees or inside in the cosy rooms, either way you can look forward to some good Mediterranean dishes. *129 Main St | tel. 02 18 63 39 80 | Budget*

PROVIANT

Perfect stop if you want to try *boerekos* – traditional cuisine of the Afrikaner people. *54 Main Rd | tel. 02 18 63 09 40 | Budget*

WHERE TO STAY

PONTAC MANOR

One of the town's oldest farmhouses is now an elegant and gracious hotel that is set in a garden surrounded by old oak trees. *23 rooms | 16 Zion St | tel. 02 18 72 04 45 | www.pontac.com | Moderate*

RODEBERG LODGE

Reasonably priced, small guest house in a restored Victorian building. *6 rooms | 74 Main St | tel. 02 18 72 08 60 | www.rodeberglodge.co.za | Budget*

INFORMATION

PAARL TOURISM BUREAU

216 Main St | tel. 02 18 63 49 37 | www.paarlonline.com

WHERE TO GO

WELLINGTON (126 B5) (*D8*)

This small sleepy town (pop. 35,000) was founded in 1837 and is characterised by its Victorian architecture. Today the *Wellington Wine Route* is growing in popularity as a route. On the historical wine estate INSIDER TIP *Doolhof* the manor house has been converted into the Grand Dédale country hotel. A paradise for horseback riders, fishermen, sports and wine enthusiasts *(7 rooms | Rustenburg Rd | tel. 02 18 73 40 89 | www.granddedale.com | Moderate). 20km (12.4mi) from Paarl*

WILDERER'S DISTILLERY (126 B5) (*D8*)

A small farm between Paarl and Franschhoek that produces some of the Cape's

Enormous barrels in the KWV wine cellar – the country's largest wine producer

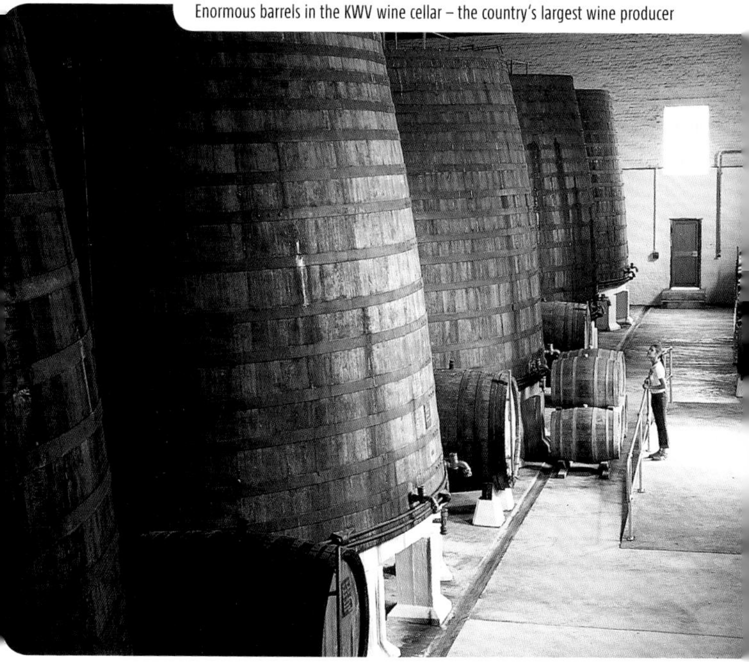

best grappa *(daily 10am–5pm)*. Restaurant serves light lunches *(on the R 45 | tel. 02 18 63 35 55 | Budget)*. *7km (4.3mi) from Paarl*

STELLEN-BOSCH

(126 B5) (D8) ★ **Stellenbosch (population of 100,000) is in South Africa's most import wine producing region, and the historic old town centre is particularly charming.**

South Africa's second oldest town's name goes back to Simon van der Stel, who started a settlement here in 1679. A stroll through the town's oak lined streets will take you straight back in time. The historical centre of town with its well-preserved Cape Dutch and Victorian buildings has a special atmosphere. Today it is a popular university town.

SIGHTSEEING

DORP STREET ●

Artistic gables are the trademark of this street's listed Cape Dutch houses. The 1851 Lutheran church today houses the university art gallery. *Oom Samie se Winkel* is a village store that is run today as it was yesteryear. Selling traditional sweets and old-fashioned food items, bric-a-brac and even antiquities. Light meals served in the garden *(84 Dorp St | tel. 02 18 83 83 79 | Budget)*.

VILLAGE MUSEUM

It comprises four houses each showcasing the lifestyle of Stellenbosch's citizen from the 18th to the mid 19th century. Built in 1710 the *Schreuderhuis* is South Africa's oldest town house, while *Blettermanhuis* is typical of the style in 1760 to 1780. The neo-classic double storey *Grosvenor House* represents the first decade of the 19th century, while *Om Bergh House* was home to the Marthinus Bergh family that lived here around the 1850s. *18 Ryneveld St | Mon–Sat 9.30am–5pm, Sun 2–5pm | entrance fee 15 rand*

FOOD & DRINK

INSIDER TIP CAPE TO CUBA

Trendy restaurant that is particularly popular among students. *13 Andringa St | tel. 02 18 87 35 59 | Budget*

INSIDER TIP CHRISTOPHE'S

Top chef Christophe Dahosse only uses fresh ingredients for his fine French dishes, cuisine in a class of its own. *44 Ryneveld St | tel. 02 18 86 87 63 | Moderate*

WIJNHUIS

A restaurant and wine bar in the heart of the town in an historic building. An extensive wine list. You can also taste wines as well as purchase from their wine shop. *Church St/Andringa St | tel. 02 18 87 58 44 | Moderate*

SHOPPING

BOEZAART BAUERMEISTER

Delicate lace-inspired fine jewellery by two female designers. *Corner Ryneveld St/ Church St*

SMAC ART GALLERY

Sells cutting-edge contemporary South African art. *De Wet Centre | Church St*

ENTERTAINMENT

TERRACE

Wednesday nights draw the biggest crowd at this student pub hotspot. Corner *Alexander St/Bird St*

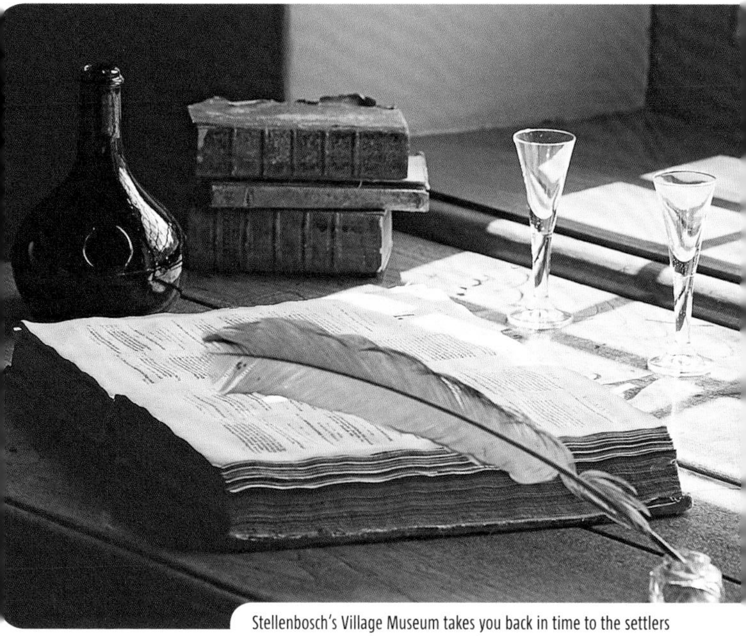

Stellenbosch's Village Museum takes you back in time to the settlers

WHERE TO STAY

BATAVIA BOUTIQUE HOTEL

Stylish guest house with a small swimming pool and a rather impressive art collection. *5 rooms | 12 Louw St | tel. 02 18 87 29 14 | www.batavia-stellenbosch.co.za | Budget*

INSIDER TIP **COOPMANHUIJS BOUTIQUE HOTEL**

This lovely town house dates back to 1713 and is now a centrally located boutique hotel. *14 rooms | 33 Church St | tel. 02 18 83 82 07 | www.coopmanhuijs.co.za | Moderate*

INFORMATION

STELLENBOSCH TOURISM

36 Market St | tel. 02 18 83 35 84 | www.stellenboschtourism.co.za

WHERE TO GO

MEERLUST (126 B5) (*D8*)

Wine estate owned by the Myburgh family that produces excellent red wines and a rather fine Chardonnay. The buildings are an excellent example of Cape Dutch. One of the many wine estates open to the public for wine tastings *(tel. 02 18 43 35 87 | www.meerlust.com). 15km (9⅓mi) from Stellenbosch*

STELLENBOSCH WINE ROUTE (126 B5–6) (*D8*)

A paradise for fine wine connoisseurs, 114 estates in Stellenbosch and surrounds offer wine tasting *(info: Stellenbosch Wine Route | 36 Market St | tel. 02 18 86 43 10 | www.wineroute.co.za)*. For organised tours contact *Vineyard Ventures (tel. 02 14 34 88 88 | www.vineyardventures.co.za)*.

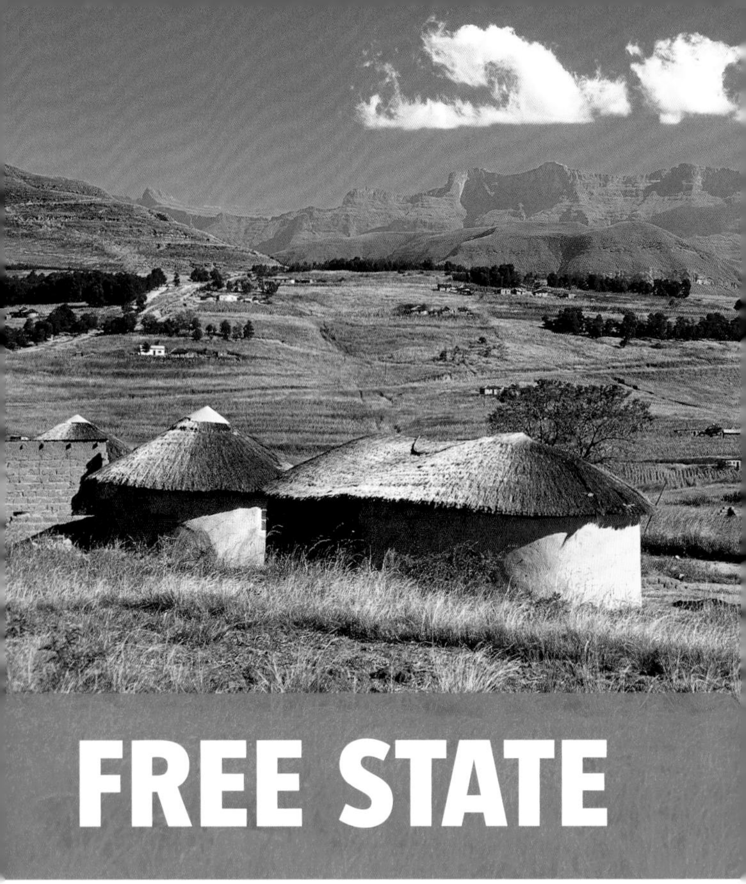

FREE STATE

The Free State is surrounded by the Northern Province, KwaZulu-Natal and the Cape Provinces. While Natal is very English, the Free State takes pride in its Afrikaans heritage.

Located on a high plateau, the province is predominantly flat and covered in maize fields and grasslands that seem to stretch on forever. Yet there is variety in its landscape. The mountain ranges in the east are snow capped in the winter and the highlands route between Harrismith in the north-east and Zastron in the south is a scenic wonder with spectacular views and ancient cave paintings from its prehistoric past. Nelson Mandela described the province in his autobiography: 'The Free State landscape gladdens my heart, no matter what my mood. When I am here I feel that nothing can shut me in and that my thoughts can roam as far as the horizons.'

Trek Boers founded the Free State after having crossed the Orange River, the province took its name from the crossing and was known as the Orange Free State until the end of the apartheid era. The early settlers were very pious and gave their new land biblical names. So there is the town of Bethlehem and a river they called the Jordan. In the same area, at the foot of the Maluti Mountains, is the

Photo: Zulu rondavel village

Farmland in the heart of South Africa: rolling grasslands and wheat farms, adventure hikes and nature reserves, all high above sea level

Golden Gate Highlands National Park with its striking and imposing sandstone cliff formations.

Hidden high up in the mountains is *Qwa-Qwa*. With its lofty mountain peaks and gently undulating meadows at a height of more than 2000m (6561ft) it is an area straight out of a story book. Home to the Basotho people, it is a landscape made for hiking. This mountain nation is famed for its handicrafts and their exquisitely woven woollen rugs and blankets that make ideal keepsakes.

In the north east of the Free State lies the Riemland. The dubious name goes back to when the Boers slaughtered the large herds of wildebeest that roamed here. Their hides were cut into narrow strips called *riempies* which were dried and used to make furniture. Aside from the

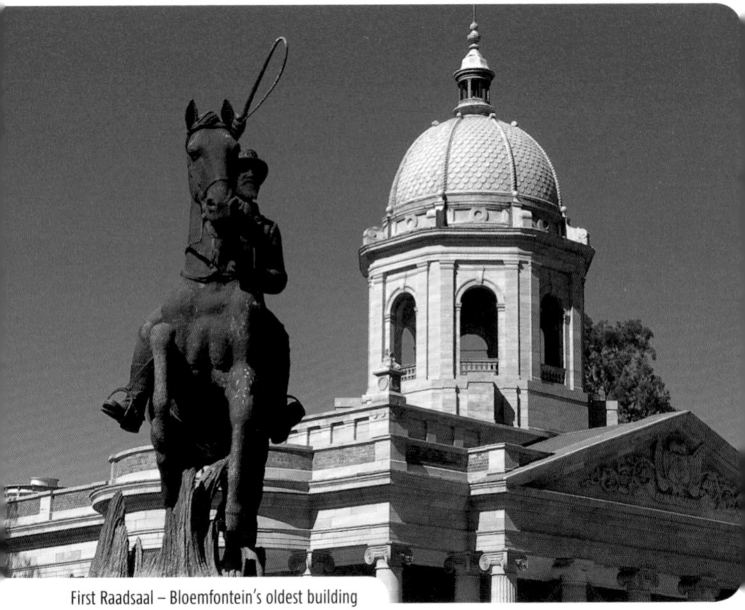

First Raadsaal – Bloemfontein's oldest building

national park, there are now also many private game farms – easy to spot because of their extra high game fences – that farm animals like springbok. In the middle of the province is its *goldfields*, an area of 127mi² that is considered to the world's richest producing gold area. More than a third of South Africa's gold is mined here.

The first traces of the precious metal were discovered in 1903 but prospecting only began 30 years later. It was after World War II that the *Anglo American Corporation* invested millions of dollars in extensive drilling operations and geological studies. Since then the area has become the centre of a state-of-the-art mining industry.

It is via Ladybrand that you reach the independent nation of Lesotho. A country surrounded by South Africa and known as the 'kingdom in the sky'. The 'kingdom' because it is a monarchy with King Letsie III as its ruler and 'sky' because it is one of the few countries in the world that lies 1000m (3280ft) above sea level.

BLOEMFONTEIN

(128 B2) (*H5*) **Bloemfontein (population of 450,000) is the capital of the Free State and seat of the Supreme Court of Appeal – the highest appeal court in South Africa.**

'The city of roses' is what Bloemfontein is popularly known because of the abundance of blooms in its gardens and parks. The fact that it is 1400m (4593ft) above sea level means that both its summers and winters are mild. Its history goes back to 1840 when Voortrekker Johannes Nicholas Brits settled here. He named his farm after what he could see around him:

CITY **WHERE TO START?**
Head to **Herzog Square** in the centre of the city where all the main sites are; the city hall, the National Museum and the Fourth Raadsaal. The Supreme Court of Appeal is on President Brand Street, which also leads to the First Raadsaal. Your best bet for parking is on President Brand Street.

a water spring surrounded by flowers. Over the years the city has become a melting pot of British and Boer influences.

SIGHTSEEING

FIRST RAADSAAL
Bloemfontein's oldest building, dating back to 1848, is where the foundations were laid for the Free State's government, church and education. *St Georges Street | Mon–Fri 10.15am–3pm, Sat/Sun 2–5pm*

NATIONAL MUSEUM
It houses an extensive fossil collection, interesting archaeological finds and showcases the Free State's history. *Aliwal St | Mon–Sat 10am–5pm, Sun noon–5.30pm | entrance fee 5 rand*

FOOD & DRINK

MEEL
Homemade bread served with tapas or tender lamb roast with some local side dishes. *87 A Kellner St | tel. 05 14 48 88 36 | Budget*

THE RAJ
Stylish restaurant serving authentic Indian cuisine. *Windmill Casino and Entertainment Centre | Jan Pierewit Rd | tel. 05 14 21 00 34 | Moderate*

SEVEN ON KELLNER
A fine dining experience that offers an interesting fusion of North African and Mediterranean dishes. *7 Kellner St | tel. 05 14 47 79 28 | Expensive*

WHERE TO STAY

DE OUDE KRAAL
Bloemfontein's finest hotel is 35km (21.7mi) south of the city. The owners have opened a guest house on their sheep farm, surrounded by 2500 acres of park and farm lands. Its restaurant also comes highly recommended. *13 rooms | N 1 exit Riversford | tel. 05 15 64 06 36 | www.deoudekraal.com | Moderate*

HOBBIT BOUTIQUE HOTEL
This small hotel has been named after the city's most famous son: author John Ronald Reuel Tolkien and his hobbit characters from *Lord of the Rings*. Not to be missed: the three-course evening set menu. *9 rooms | 19 President Steyn Ave | tel. 05 14 47 06 63 | www.hobbit.co.za | Budget*

INFORMATION

BLOEMFONTEIN TOURISM
60 Park St | tel. 05 14 05 84 90 | www.bloemfonteintourism.co.za

MARCO POLO HIGHLIGHTS

★ **Golden Gate Highlands National Park**
Impressive sandstone cliffs
→ p. 70

★ **Lesotho**
Independent mountain kingdom right in the middle of South Africa
→ p. 71

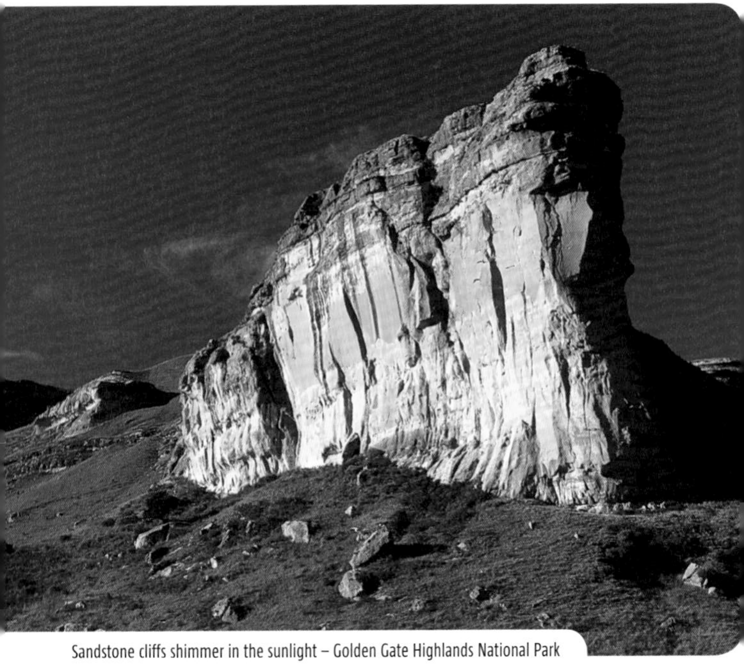

Sandstone cliffs shimmer in the sunlight – Golden Gate Highlands National Park

WHERE TO GO

INSIDER TIP BASOTHO CULTURAL VILLAGE ● (128 C2) *(K5)*
Just 20km (12.4mi) east of the main entrance to the Golden Gate Highlands National Park is this outdoor museum. It gives insights into how the Basotho have lived for centuries. Basotho women in traditional garb welcome visitors into their traditional thatched huts. *Mon–Fri 8am–4.30pm, Sat/Sun 8.30am–5pm | entrance fee including tour 20 rand | 200km (124mi) from Bloemfontein*

CLARENS (128 C2) *(K5)*
This village is a little jewel and the perfect place to stop over on your way to the Basotho Cultural Village. There is a thriving artist community and you can see their works at the Art and Wine Gallery on Main Street. *Lake Clarens Guest House (4 rooms | 401 Church St | tel. 058256 1436 | Budget)* is a good overnight option and for dinner *Clementines* restaurant comes highly recommended *(Main St | tel. 0582561616 | Moderate). 240km (149mi) from Bloemfontein*

GOLDEN GATE HIGHLANDS NATIONAL PARK ★ (128 C2) *(K5)*
The park owes its name to the spectacular sandstone cliffs that shimmer gold when the sun catches them. Made up of an area of 46mi² in the rolling foothills of the Maluti Mountains, it is home to local game and there are also eagles that nest high up in the mountains.
There are two overnight camps in the park where you can rent a rondavel or cottage

and a hotel, the *Golden Gate Hotel (20 rooms | Budget). R 49 between Bethlehem and Harrismith | tel. 05 82 55 10 00 | 180km (112mi) from Bloemfontein | entrance fee 76 rand*

LADYBRAND (128 B1) (*J5*)
Located on the Lesotho border this town is surrounded by the majestic *Maluti Mountains.* It is characterised by old sandstone houses that line its exceptionally wide streets. Ladybrand was founded in 1867 as an Afrikaner defence post against the Basotho. Today this town enjoys extensive trade with its Lesotho neighbours. *Villa on Joubert* B & B harks back to the pioneer days when the town first came into being *(5 rooms | 47 Joubert St | tel. 05 19 24 18 14 | www.villaonjoubert.com | Budget).*

LESOTHO ★
(128–129 B–D 2–3) (*J–K 5–6*)
This independent kingdom in the midst of mountain country is about the size of Belgium. Home to the Basotho since the beginning of the 19th century, the 'roof of Africa' has a magnificent landscape but is still very underdeveloped in terms of a tourist infrastructure. The 20km (12.4mi) long, 1300m (4265ft) high *Sani Pass* is the only road between Lesotho and KwaZulu-Natal and is only suitable for four-wheel drive vehicles.
The most comfortable accommodation in *Maseru* is at the *Lesotho Sun (210 rooms | tel. 0 92 66 22 24 30 00 | www.sunintern national.com | Moderate).* The *Malealea Lodge (20 rooms| tel. 08 25 52 45 15 | Budget)* lies in an isolated valley in the western part of the kingdom and offers rondavel accommodation in stunning surrounds. It is the ideal spot from where to set out on a pony trek into the mountains *(from Maseru via Motsekuoa to Malealea).* You can buy traditional woven Basotho straw hats in all of the street markets in Lesotho. This traditional pointed headwear is called the *mokorotlo* and it the country's national symbol. In 2006 the country changed their national flag and replaced the warlike symbols with a stylized Basotho hat. *120km (74mi) from Bloemfontein*

WELKOM
(128 B1) (*J4*)
Welkom is the pulse of the goldfields. The fact that this town was planned on the drawing board is still evident today. There are no traffic lights, very few stop streets – plenty of traffic circles. The *Red Ox Restaurant (Graaff St | tel. 05 73 52 85 05 | Budget)* is very popular. An exciting adventure is a day tour of a gold mine. Tours must be booked in advance through *Welkom Tourism (tel. 05 73 52 92 44).* Welkom is also home to numerous bird species with flamingos visible in the lakes around the town. *180km (112mi) from Bloemfontein*

LOW BUDGET

▶ Afrikaans, the language of the Boers, is the world's youngest language. You can find out more at the *National Afrikaans Literature Museum* in Bloemfontein. *President Brand St | admission free*

▶ All-inclusive horseback riding through a nature reserve in the mountain range bordering Lesotho: for as little as 1000 rand for two days. You will stay in a mountain hut overnight. Your bedding and provisions are carried by an accompanying off-road vehicle. *Bokpoort Farm near Clarens | tel. 05 82 56 11 81 | www.bokpoort.co.za | Budget*

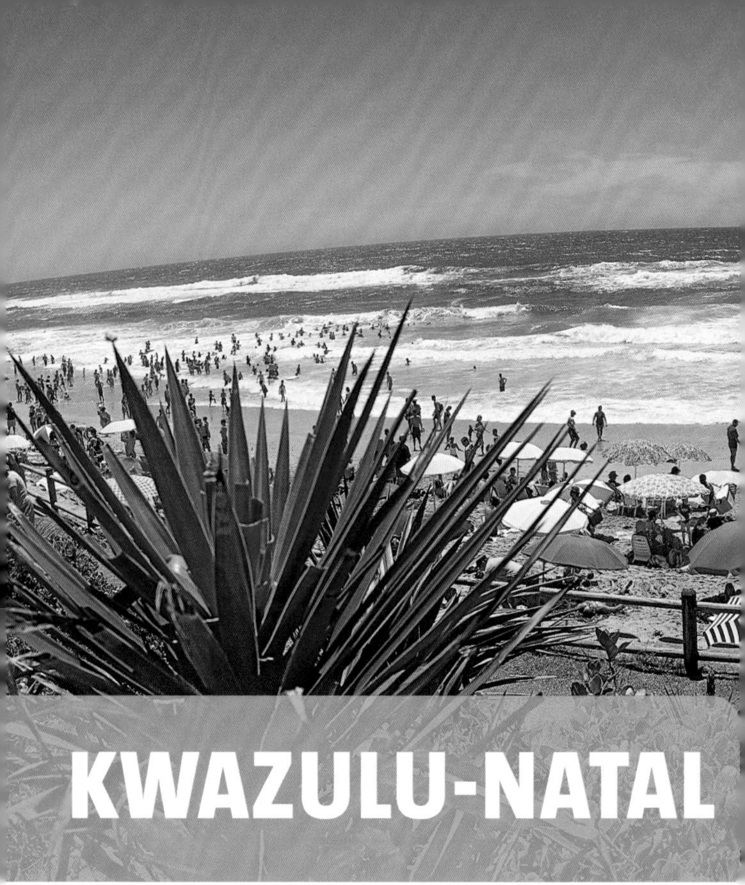

KWAZULU-NATAL

The beauty and diversity of this small province's landscape is most impressive. Typical African veldt characterises the north while the coastal areas along the Indian Ocean has a subtropical climate. The province boast stunning beaches, lush green vegetation, rolling countryside crisscrossed by rivers and one of the world's most spectacular mountain ranges, the Drakensberg.

The eclectic mix of European, Afrikaans, Asian and Zulu cultures have all had an influence, making this a fascinating province. A large part of it formed the Zulu kingdom from 1820 to 1880. The descendants of the famed Zulu warriors, Shaka and Dingaan, still live here today. The fearless reputation of their leaders spread far beyond their borders. The Voortrekkers reached what was then called Natal in 1838. Their laager was attacked by the Zulus and several hundred people were killed. The Boers took revenge and defeated the Zulus at the Battle of Blood River. The victorious Boers declared a republic but by 1843 it was in British control.

DURBAN

(129 E3) (*L6*) **With its wide, white sandy beaches on the Indian Ocean,**

Photo: Life is a beach – Umhlanga Rocks

Home of the Zulu nation: its beautiful Indian Ocean beaches and magnificent mountain ranges offer visitors plenty of variety

Durban (population of 3.5 million) is one of South Africa's top holiday destinations. The sun shines here for 300 days a year and visitors to this vibrant port city will find it hard to believe that as recently 150 years ago there was nothing here but wild jungle. The Zulus still call the city *eThekwini* or 'the quiet lagoon'.

At the end of 1497 Vasco da Gama came across this piece of paradise while en route

> CITY **WHERE TO START?**
> The **Golden Mile** is a 6km (3.7mi) long beach promenade on the Marine Parade. It starts at South Beach, passes the World Cup stadium and stretches all the way to the Point – the harbour entrance. You should find parking on Ordnance Road.

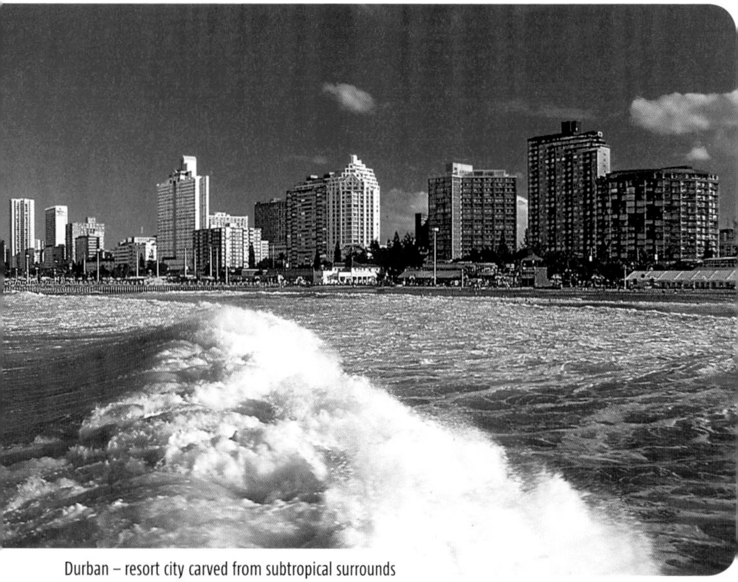

Durban – resort city carved from subtropical surrounds

to Asia. As it was on Christmas he called it Natal, the Portuguese word for Christmas. It was only in 1835 that it was renamed Durban after Sir Benjamin D'Urban, who was governor of the Cape in the mid 19th century. Many of Durban's inhabitants are descendants of the workforce that the then colonial British rulers brought in from India to tend the sugar plantations. Durban's Indian markets, mosques and stores all bear testimony to this past and form part of the cultural melting pot that makes Durban so attractive today. Its harbour is South Africa's largest and it is the heartbeat of the city.

SIGHTSEEING

KWAMULE MUSEUM

The Kwamule Museum is completely devoted to South Africa's more recent history which is why it is often referred to as the Apartheid Museum. *130 Ordinance Rd | Mon–Sat 8.30am–3.30pm, Sun 11.30am–4pm | admission free*

MOSES MABHIDA STADIUM ★

Many regard this as the most beautiful of the stadiums built for the 2010 Soccer World Cup. A 350m (1148ft) long and 106m (347ft) high arch spans the stadium. Visitors can walk across it *(entrance 80 rand)* or take the cable car *(entrance 50 rand)* and the adventurous can *bungee jump* from the highest point for 595 rand. *9am–6pm daily*

USHAKA MARINE WORLD

This aquarium and marine theme park is Africa's largest and has a distinctly Disneyland feel to it. On display are more than 1000 fish species in elaborately designed aquariums. The popular dolphin show runs three times a day at 10.30am, 1.30pm and 3.30pm. *At the harbour on Point Rd | entrance 104 rand*

FOOD & DRINK

CAFÉ 1999
Small restaurant with delicious mains and delectable desserts. *Shop 2, Silvervause Centre | Silverton Rd | Berea | tel. 03 12 02 34 06* | Budget

HARVEY'S RESTAURANT
Classical dishes and a stylish atmosphere. *465 Innes Rd | Morningside | tel. 03 13 12 57 06* | Expensive

ROMA REVOLVING RESTAURANT
A stunning 360 degree view of the Durban cityscape and top notch Mediterranean cuisine. *John Ross House, 22nd floor | Victoria Embankment | tel. 03 13 37 67 07* | Moderate

INSIDER TIP SILVERANI'S
Indian curry and the city's best *'bunny chows': a* half a loaf of bread filled with curry, a meal unique to KwaZulu-Natal. *Silvervause Centre | Silverton Rd | Berea |tel. 03 12 01 50 88* | Budget

SHOPPING

AFRICAN ART CENTRE
Arts and crafts by Zulu artists. *94 Florida Road*

VICTORIA STREET MARKET
Some 180 stalls selling spices, fish, meat, jewellery etc. but also an eclectic mix of African and Indian goods. *Victoria St*

SPORTS & ACTIVITIES

The *Windsor Park Golf Club* boasts a 9-hole and an 18-hole golf course *(tel. 03 13 12 73 54)*. Swim with the dolphins with *Calypso Dive (tel. 03 13 32 09 05)*. Harbour cruises depart from the harbour's *Pleasure Cruise Terminal*.

ENTERTAINMENT

CZAR
Durban's party mile is on *Florida Road* and that is also where you will find Czar. This club, restaurant and tapas bar is the city's trendiest nightclub. *178 Florida Rd*

MOYO USHAKA BAR ●
No better spot in Durban for a sundowner. This chic, designer bar is at the end of the uShaka Pier only a few feet above the breakers. *1 Bell Street*

WHERE TO STAY

EDWARD HOTEL
Elegant hotel with a brilliant view of the Indian Ocean. *240 rooms | 149 O.R. Tambo Parade | tel. 03 13 37 36 81 | switchboard@proteaedward.co.za* | Moderate

ESSENWOOD HOUSE
A small Victorian hotel high above Durban in the suburb of Berea, just a few miles from the city. *7 rooms | 630 Essenwood*

MARCO POLO HIGHLIGHTS

★ **Moses Mabhida Stadium**
An architectural success – right on the Indian Ocean → p. 74

★ **Umhlanga Rocks**
Popular Indian Ocean resort town → p. 77

★ **Valley of a Thousand Hills**
Magnificent views of undulating hills and valleys → p. 77

★ **Drakensberg**
South Africa's 'Alps' – an experience not just for mountaineers and hikers → p. 79

World Heritage Site – iSimangaliso Lucia Wetland Park on the Indian Ocean

Rd | tel. 0312074547 | www.essenwood house.co.za | Budget

QUARTERS ON FLORIDA

Superbly run hotel. The charming rooms come with bouquets of flowers and home-made biscuits. *23 rooms | 101 Florida Rd | Morningside | tel. 0313035246 | www.quarters.co.za* | Moderate

LOW BUDGET

▶ The Durban Art Gallery was South Africa's first art gallery to buy the works of black artists. The collection is most impressive and admission is free.

▶ Entrance to the vibrant retail centre Village Walk – with its typically African market theme – inside the uShaka Marine World theme park in Durban, is free of charge. Accessible from the parking area you will also be able to look out on to the underwater aquarium, the world's fifth largest, and the shark enclosures, where visitors can dive with the sharks.

INFORMATION

DURBAN TOURISM

160 Pine St | tel. 0313044934 | www.durban.kzn.org.za

WHERE TO GO

HLUHLUWE UMFOLOZI PARK

(129 E–F 1–2) (*M L–M 4–5*)

This is the only place in KwaZulu-Natal where you will get to see the *Big Five*. In existence since 1895 and covering an area of 370mi², this stunning game reserve is South Africa's oldest. *Nov–Feb 5am–7pm daily, March–Oct 6am–6pm daily | entrance fee 80 rand | 180km (69mi) from Durban*

ISIMANGALISO WETLAND PARK

(129 E–F 1–2) (*M M4–5*)

Boasting five ecosystems – lakes, ocean, dunes, savannah and wetlands – this park stretches along the Indian Ocean coast and has been declared a Unesco World Heritage site *(Oct–March 5am–8pm daily, April–Sept 6am–8pm daily)*. In the north of the park, 180km (112mi) from Durban is the INSIDER TIP *Thonga Beach Lodge*. Guests get to stay on an isolated stretch of beach in luxurious thatched rondavels

(24 rooms | tel. 03 54 74 14 73 | www.isibindiafrica.co.za | Moderate).

SWAZILAND
(125 E–F 4–5) (*L–M 3–4*)

From Durban take the N 2 north for 300km (186mi) and you will reach the tiny, independent kingdom of Swaziland. The capital is *Mbabane* and the royal residence is in the *Ezulwini Valley.* You can stay over at the king's guest house INSIDER TIP *Royal Villas (68 rooms | tel. 09268 4 16 70 35 | www.royalvillasswaziland.com | Moderate).* Swaziland is the second smallest country (after Gambia) in Africa. It has six scenic national parks. *Big Game Parks | tel. 09 26 85 28 39 44 | www.biggameparks.org*

UMHLANGA ROCKS ★
(129 E3) (*L5*)

Perfect for that beach holiday, this resort town on the Indian Ocean lies some 20km (12mi) north-east of Durban. The hotels here are all right on the beach. The newly refurbished INSIDER TIP *Oysterbox Hotel (86 rooms | Lighthouse Rd | tel. 03 15 61 22 33 | www.oysterboxhotel.co.za | Expensive)* comes highly recommended. Another little piece of paradise is *Zimbali Lodge* in *Ballito,* some 30km (18mi) north of Durban. Situated above the Dolphin Coast and surrounded by natural subtropical vegetation it offers exclusive accommodation and top class meals. There is also an 18-hole golf course *(76 rooms | tel. 03 17 65 44 46 | www.zimbali.org | Expensive).*

VALLEY OF A THOUSAND HILLS ★
(129 E2) (*L5*)

Your best view of the expansive, undulating hills and valleys is from Botha's Hill *(Information: 1000 Hills Tourism | tel. 03 17 77 18 74 | www.1000hills.kzn.org.za).* Watch traditional Zulu dancing in a kraal at the *Phezulu Safari Park (8.30am–4.30pm daily | entrance fee 65 rand | 30km (18mi) from Durban).*

Giraffes in the Hluhluwe Umfolozi Park

Zulu in traditional gear

PIETER-MARITZBURG

(129 E2) (*🗺 L5*) **Tucked in a valley and surrounded by rolling green hills, is Pietermaritzburg (pop. 45,000) a city with a Victorian historic centre that is a testament to its colonial British heritage.** Despite the obvious British legacy, the town was in fact founded by Voortrekkers who also left behind their influences. They founded the Republic of Natalia, with Pietermaritzburg as its capital, named after leaders Piet Retief and Gerrit Maritz.

SIGHTSEEING

HOWICK FALLS

Here the Umgeni River plunges 111m (364ft) over a spectacular gorge. *On the road to Howick, 15km (9.3mi)*

TATHAM ART GALLERY ●

A significant collection of contemporary South African art as well as some international and European masters. *Commercial Rd | Tue–Sun 10am–4pm | admission free*

FOOD & DRINK

INSIDER TIP EATON'S ON EIGHTY

Small but select menu, try the highly recommended lamb dishes. *80 Roberts Rd | tel. 03 33 42 32 80 | Moderate*

ROSEHURST

Light, fresh meals and delicious home baked rye bread. *239 Boom St | tel. 03 33 94 38 83 | Budget*

WHERE TO STAY

INSIDER TIP BRIAR GHYLL LODGE

Victorian manor house surrounded by a huge park 5km (3mi) outside the city. *8 rooms | George Macfarlane Lane | tel. 03 33 42 26 64 | www.bglodge.co.za | Moderate*

FORDOUN HOTEL & SPA ●

On the outskirts of the city is Fordoun, one of South Africa's best spas. The *sangoma* or traditional healer prepares oils and tinctures from the some 120 plants found in the gardens. *17 rooms | Nottingham Rd | tel. 03 32 66 62 17 | www.fordoun.com | Moderate*

INFORMATION

PIETERMARITZBURG TOURISM
177 Commercial Rd | tel. 03 33 45 13 48 | www.pmbtourism.co.za

WHERE TO GO

DRAKENSBERG ★
(128–129 C–E 1–3) (*J–L 4–6*)
The view you get of the northern Drakensberg from the *Royal Natal National Park* is breathtaking – before you in all its glory is the rock face called the Amphitheatre. Stay over in the *Orion Mount-Aux-Sources Hotel | 107 rooms | tel. 03 64 38 80 00 | www.oriongroup.co.za | Moderate*. In the centre of the Drakensberg mountain range is *Giant's Castle Game Reserve* with its dramatic rock formations and diversity of plant and wildlife. En route to the neighbouring *Kamberg Nature Reserve* you will find the small INSIDER TIP *Cleopatra Mountain Farmhouse (11 rooms | tel. 03 32 67 99 00 | www.cleomountain.com | Expensive)* hotel. Guests are treated to a select menu every evening. *80km (50mi) from Pietermaritzburg*

INSIDER TIP MIDLANDS MEANDER
(129 D2) (*K5*)
The picturesque area surrounding *Nottingham Road* is an artists' haven. Some 150 artists, craftsmen and restaurants form part of the 60km (37mi) route between Pietermaritzburg and Mooi River and are open to the general public to visit. Well signposted, participating galleries and studios are easy to find to the right and left of the N 3. *www.midlandsmeander.co.za | 50km (31mi) from Pietermaritzburg*

Impressive Howick Falls – Umgeni Valley Nature Reserve

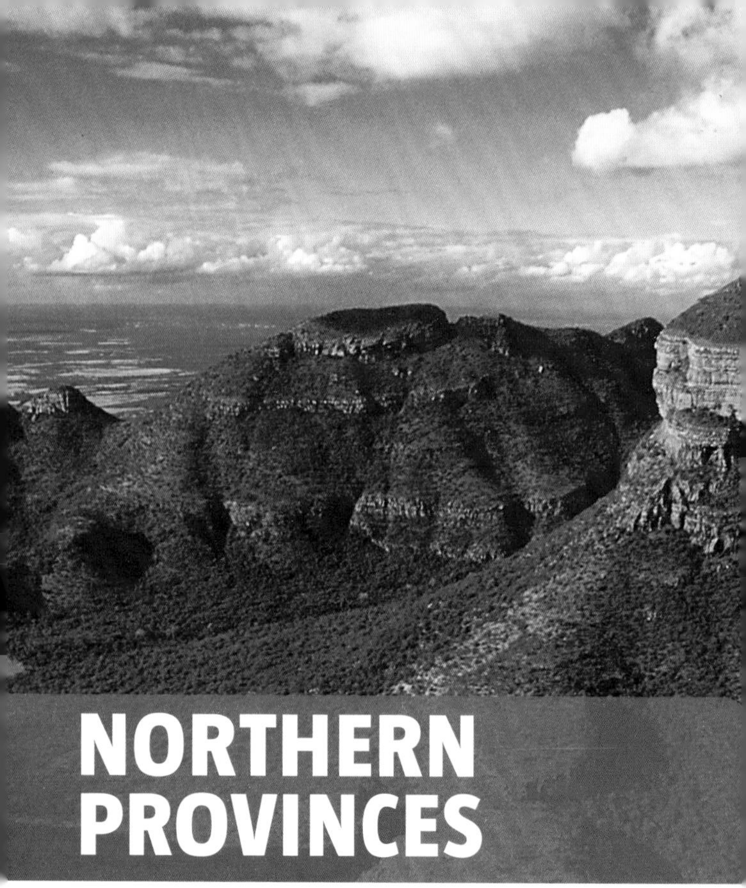

NORTHERN PROVINCES

When you jet into Johannesburg International Airport in the morning you know you have arrived in Africa: the dry Highveld air, the reddish steppe-like grasslands that seem to go on forever, the bright blue sky and the breathtakingly beautiful sunrise.

This was the last part of South Africa that the white settlers colonised. Johannesburg is only just over a century old, while neighbouring Pretoria, today a suburb of Tshwane, only a few decades older. The Great North Road begins north of Pretoria, making its way through hilly grassland terrain to Bela-Bela (formerly Warmbaths), a northern Sotho word meaning 'boiling place'. It is named for the hot springs that erupt from the ground here at 63 degrees Celsius. From here the road takes you hundreds of kilometres via Waterberg and Polokwane through baobab terrain across the Soutpansberg Mountains to the Limpopo River (that forms the border to Zimbabwe and Botswana). Travelling through this unspoilt part of Africa is an unforgettable experience. Only recently some very rare plants and birds were discovered in a valley of the isolated Venda Mountains.

The most interesting province in the north has to be Mpumalanga. Here settlers discovered gold before the rush began on

Photo: Blyde River Canyon

Formerly the Transvaal – and once synonymous with Johannesburg and Pretoria – it is has now been divided into several provinces

the Witwatersrand. Pilgrim's Rest was pivotal to the early gold rush and today it is a living museum, a listed town and a tourist attraction. What make this province so impressive are its countless lookout points with views over its unusual landscape and spectacular waterfalls. In Mpumalanga the inland plateau experiences a dramatic drop of more than 1000m (3280ft) to a subtropical level. This dramatic landscape of misty mountains and waterfalls is what you will discover on the Panorama Route.

A highlight of the route is a drive along the Blyde River Canyon and the renowned God's Window lookout point. From here you get to look down 700m (2296ft) on to the Lowveld with its canyons, ravines, rock formations (dating back millions of years) and winding rivers. At the end of the route is Nelspruit, the region's largest town. From here it is not far to the northernmost gate of the world famous Kruger National Park.

The northern provinces (the Orange Free State and Transvaal) were founded by the Voortrekkers who fled from the Cape and the British in the mid 19th century. No sooner were diamonds discovered and the British wanted to convince their former opponents to enter into a confederation with them. When this failed, they annexed the republics. This sparked the beginning of the first Anglo-Boer War or *Vryheidsoorlog* as it is known in Afrikaans. The Boers were the victors in this dispute and in 1881 the Transvaal regained its independence. The country quickly developed under the leadership of the legendary President Paul Kruger, referred to as 'Oom Paul'. When a huge gold discovery was made near Pretoria in 1886 he was well aware of the problems that it would bring with it. The discovery could not be kept secret and the resultant gold rush attracted thousands of fortune seekers from around the world.

The British had become resolute in their intention to capture this part of southern Africa for themselves. The Second Boer War broke out with Britain emerging victorious in 1902. In 1910 the South African Republic was founded – with Pretoria as its administrative capital. Today Pretoria, in the Tshwane municipality, remains the seat of government. Since 1994 it has been the residency of the ANC presidents and their governments and, like their National Party predecessors, they are sworn in here.

The area where the gold was discovered is called the Witwatersrand. It is a 1700m (5577ft) high plateau with a gold-bearing vein that stretches for more than 130km (80mi) widening to 30km (18mi) towards the end it. It is an area of mining and industrial towns – the largest being Johannesburg which is the economic power-

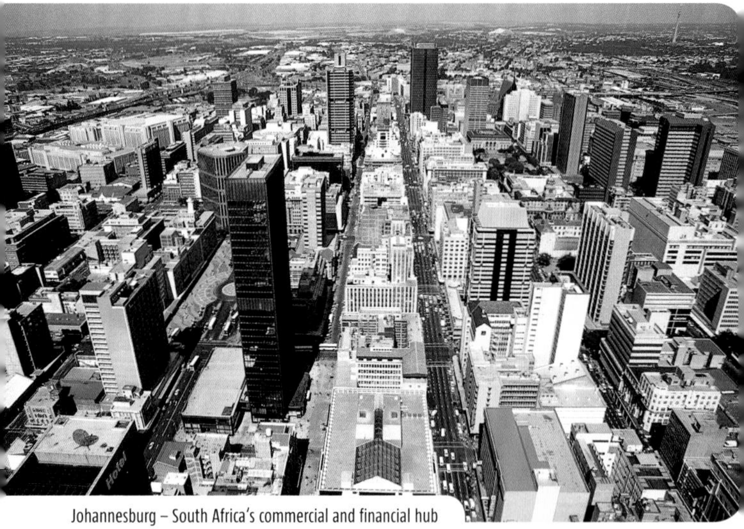

Johannesburg – South Africa's commercial and financial hub

house of Africa. The Vaal River is a favourite weekend spot for Johannesburg residents. If they do not own a second home there, they will hire a cottage or check into one of the many fine hotels dotted along its banks.

The university town Potchefstroom north of Johannesburg founded in1838 was the first capital of the South African Republic. Many of its buildings date back to this time. North West Province is one of the poorest provinces and its tourism potential has not been fully explored but it is home to Sun City and the Palace of the Lost City – known as the Las Vegas of South Africa – and two massive nature reserves: Pilansberg and Madikwe. Despite this, very few people take the trouble to visit Rustenburg in the land of the Bafokeng or the Magaliesberg Mountains, said to be a hundred times older than the Himalayas.

JOHANNESBURG

MAP ON P. 130

(J–K3) **With a population pushing well past the six million mark Johannesburg is South Africa's largest city, and even if its location cannot compete with Cape Town, it has its own unique charm.** The atmosphere is electric and the lifestyle fast paced, at times so reckless that it is still feels like its pioneer days as a mining town. Everything revolves around money and business. Johannesburg is the country's commercial and financial capital and the home of the stock exchange, a massive airport, the widest streets and the tallest skyscrapers in the country. Since the World Cup it also has the high speed Gautrain that takes commuters from Sandton to the airport in less than 15 minutes. During the apartheid era Sandton was the city's new more palatable residential and commercial hub while the city centre became increasingly run down. However, that has changed in recent years and today downtown Johannesburg is considered *the* place to work in, live in or go out in.

WHERE TO START?

CITY **Newtown** is Johannesburg's art and cultural centre and it is here on Bree Street that you will find the Museum Africa, the Newton Gallery, good restaurants and bars and the famous Market Theatre. The African Cultural Centre is reached via Wolhuter Street while parallel to Bree Street is Jeppe Street with the Workers' Museum. Parking is available in the Carlton Centre car park.

MARCO POLO HIGHLIGHTS

★ **Gold Reef City**
A Johannesburg theme park based on the gold rush with rides, hotels and restaurants → p. 85

★ **Sun City and the Palace of the Lost City**
Luxury entertainment oasis with hotels, casinos and sports facilities → p. 87

★ **Union Buildings**
The seat of government in Pretoria is at its best in October when the jacarandas are in bloom → p. 89

★ **Kruger National Park**
The world's most famous game reserve → p. 90

Johannesburg is a city of contrasts, where extreme wealth and utter poverty collide on a daily basis. In its history Johannesburg has reinvented itself a number of times. Property prices in some parts of the city centre are so high that it is more profitable to tear down old houses and replace them with newer, higher buildings, especially in affluent areas like Rosebank and Sandton. The properties and office buildings in exclusive suburbs are surrounded by high walls and electric fences and crime is at its highest here compared to the rest of South Africa. Black South Africans call Johannesburg *eGoli* – Zulu for 'city of gold'. It is with gold that everything began. George Harrison, an Australian prospector, recognised the gold content of the stones in 1886. What happened next has gone down in history as the greatest gold rush of all times. Gold prospectors from three continents embarked on the arduous journey south and it was from its beginning as a lager of tents and corrugated huts that the city developed into a thriving metropolis.

Apartheid Museum – for an in-depth look at South Africa's political past

SIGHTSEEING

APARTHEID MUSEUM (0) *(🗺 0)*
A must for all visitors, this museum gives visitors an overview and an understanding of South Africa's political past. *Northern Parkway | 8 Gold Reef Rd | Tue–Sun 10am–5pm | entrance fee 50 rand*

CONSTITUTION HILL (131 D2) *(🗺 0)*
South Africa's new Constitutional Court has been built next to the notorious Old Fort Prison, where Nelson Mandela served part of his time behind bars. In contrast to previous court buildings it is friendly, warm and open to the general public. The

collection of contemporary art in its museum is also well worth a visit. *Corner Hospital St/Kotze St | 9am–5pm daily | prison, court and museum tours every 30 minutes | entrance 15 rand*

GOLD REEF CITY ★ (0) (*🗺 0*)
This recreation of a gold mining town some 6km (3.7mi) south of the city centre has a theme park feel to it with restaurants, an amusement park and casino complex. Visitors can go down the mine shaft to the former *Crown Mines* below the city. *M 1 South motorway taking the Gold Reef City exit*

SOWETO (0) (*🗺 0*)
The name stands for South Western Township and a conservative estimate puts the number of people living here at two million. Soweto became world famous during the school riots that ended in bloodshed on 16 June 1976. The *Hector Peterson Museum (Ngakane St | 9.30am–4.30pm daily | entrance fee 25 rand)* has photographic exhibits of that day when 14 year old activist Hector Peterson was shot dead by police.
The *Mandela Family Museum (Ngakane St | 10am–4.30pm daily | entrance fee 20 rand)* is in the same street. This is the small house where Nelson Mandela – affectionately known to South Africans as *Madiba* – lived before his arrest in 1956. *Contact Jimmy's Face to Face Tours | tel. 0113 31 61 09 | www.face2face.co.za*

FOOD & DRINK

LE CANARD (0) (*🗺 0*)
Top chef Freda Appelbaum serves classical dishes in an opulent atmosphere in her restaurant which is often frequented by big names in politics and commerce. *153 Rivonia Rd | Sandton | tel. 0118 84 45 97 | Expensive*

GRAMADOELAS (130 B4) (*🗺 0*)
This restaurant serves the whole spectrum of South African cuisine. *Market Theatre Complex, Newtown | tel. 0118 38 69 60 | Moderate*

MOYO (0) (*🗺 0*)
An open air venue next to Zoo Lake that serves traditional African dishes in an ethnic atmosphere. Ideal spot for lunch. *1 Prince of Wales Dr | tel. 0116 46 00 58 | Moderate*

WADIE'S PLACE
(0) (*🗺 0*)
Once a Soweto *shebeen*, today traditional fare is served to diner seated at long communal tables. *618 Makhalamele St | Dube Township | tel. 0119 82 27 96 | Budget*

SHOPPING

INSIDER TIP **AFRICAN ROOFTOP MARKET** (0) (*🗺 0*)
A must for flea market fans with more than 450 stalls, from bric-a-brac to antiques, there something for everyone. *Rosebank Mall | 50 Bath Ave | Sun 9am–5pm*

INSIDER TIP **ARTS ON MAIN**
(131 F4)(*🗺 0*)
After years of neglect downtown Johannesburg has finally been discovered by the city's creative fraternity. The Arts on Main building complex has been successfully revamped and today it houses the studios of well known artists like William Kentridge, several galleries like the Bailey Seippel Gallery and designer shops like Black Coffee. *264 Fox St*

INSIDER TIP **BRYANSTON ORGANIC MARKET** (0) (*🗺 0*)
For more than 33 years organic foods, wooden toys, exotic teas and other organic products have been sold here. *Culross Rd*

ENTERTAINMENT

MARKET THEATRE
(130 B4) (*🕮 0*)
Some of South Africa's best theatre productions are performed here. This complex dedicated to the arts houses bookstores, galleries, bars and restaurants in what was the city's main fruit and vegetable market built way back in 1913. Many trendy and alternative shops and galleries can be found in the surrounding area. *Wolhuter St | tel. 0118 32 16 41*

INSIDER TIP **RANDLORDS**
(130 B2) (*🕮 0*)
This is the bar to see and be seen at. It is on the 22nd floor so there are fabulous views. The décor is a mix of *très chic* and African. *41 De Korte St | tel. 08 34 54 65 29*

WHERE TO STAY

INSIDER TIP **HOTEL LAMUNU**
(130 B2) (*🕮 0*)
Ultra modern downtown hotel with lots of orange décor as Lamunu is Sesotho for 'orange'. *60 rooms | 90 De Korte St | Morningside Manor | tel. 0112 42 86 00 | www.lamunu.co.za | Budget*

NEO'S B & B
(0) (*🕮 0*)
Small guest house in a neighbourhood where families of well known politicians – like Nelson Mandela, Desmond Tutu and Walter Sisulu – reside. *2 rooms | 8041 Bacela St | Orlando West | tel. 0115 36 04 13 | Budget*

INSIDER TIP **THE PEECH HOTEL**
(0) (*🕮 0*)
Rooms in this stylish hotel in upmarket Melrose have been designed to be environmentally friendly. Solar energy heats the water and wastewater is recycled in the garden. *16 rooms | 61 North St | tel. 0115 37 97 97 | www.thepeech.co.za | Moderate*

TEN BOMPAS (0) (*🕮 0*)
Each suite has been decorated by a different interior designer using various African themes. They all have their own fireplace and steam bath. *10 rooms | 10 Bompas Rd | Dunkeld West | tel. 0113 41 02 82 | www.tenbompas.com | Expensive*

THE WESTCLIFF (0) (*🕮 0*)
Plush hotel on the hillside above one of Johannesburg's most exclusive suburbs. *120 rooms | 69 Jan Smuts Ave | Saxonwold | tel. 0116 46 24 00 | www.westcliff.co.za | Expensive*

INFORMATION

GAUTENG TOURISM CENTRE
(130 A–B4) (*🕮 0*)
Central Place | Newtown | tel. 0116 39 16 00 | www.gauteng.net

WHERE TO GO

THE CRADLE OF HUMANKIND NATURE RESERVE ● (124 C4) (*J3*)

In 1990 this 470km² (181mi²) area was declared a Unesco World Heritage Site. It is comprised of twelve fossils sites one of which is the famed *Sterkfontein Cave*. The most famous and oldest find is *Little Foot*, a skeleton dating back 3.3 million years. The Cradle complex has a number of sections and they all charge a separate entrance fee. For more information go to *www.valleyofancestors.com* and *www.cradleofhumankind.co.za*. The entrance fee for the *Maropeng Visitor Centre* is 80 rand. The *Cradle Restaurant (Route T 3 | Kromdraai Rd | tel. 0116 59 16 22 | Budget) is also recommended.*

SUN CITY AND THE PALACE OF THE LOST CITY ★ (124 B3) (*J3*)

About two-and-a-half hours and 110km (68mi) drive from Johannesburg is South Africa's answer to Las Vegas. An entertainment area that looms out of the barren landscape like an oasis in a desert. Guests have a choice of three hotels, numerous swimming pools and sports facilities as well as an artificial lake with every conceivable water sport and an 18-hole green designed by golfing great Gary Player. Everything you see – rocks, waterfalls, palms or flamingos – is either artificial or imported. In the evening guests can choose between a number of restaurants, the casino, one-armed bandits and spectacular shows. There are also safari trips out to the nearby *Pilanesberg Game Reserve*. In the early 1990s entrepreneur Sol Kerzner opened the *The Palace of the Lost City* next to Sun City in a six acre area. This thoroughly kitsch complex emulates an age-old African mythical city and it is so over the top that it comes full circle and is a charming fantasy world with an ultra-lavish luxury hotel. Sun City has its own station and airport and the *Sun City*

Palace of the Lost City – the Las Vegas of South Africa

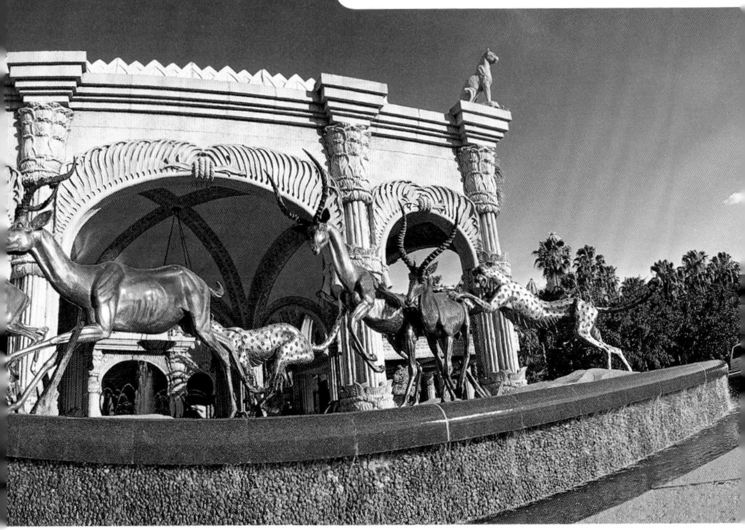

Express transports day visitors from the parking lot to the entrance of the Sun City entertainment hub *(entrance fee 70 rand | Sun City Buses operates daily to and from Johannesburg | tel. 01 45 57 44 88)*. The four hotels in Sun City itself cater for every budget and taste. Families may prefer the *Cabanas (380 rooms | tel. 01 45 57 12 72 | Budget)* while those who like luxury and kitsch should opt for *The Palace (338 rooms | tel. 01 45 57 31 31 | Expensive)*; for all the hotels on site go to: *www.suninternational.com)*.

WHERE TO START?
Burgerpark on Jacob Maré Street is a good place to set out from. Opposite is Melrose House and from here you can follow Andries Street until you get to Minaar Street and the Transvaal Museum. Opposite it is the city hall and a block away in Visagie Street is the Cultural History Museum surrounded by yet another park. Best parking options are on Pretorius Street or Andries Street.

LOW BUDGET

▶ Staying at a privately run game lodge can be expensive. An exception is the Mosetha Bush Camp in the Madikwe Game Reserve. A backpacker lodge without electricity where you get to shower under the African skies – a terrific atmosphere! *18 rooms | tel. 011 444 93 45 | www.thebushcamp.com | Budget*

▶ Museum Africa in Johannesburg covers a whole spectrum of South Africa's heritage going back to the rock art of its oldest inhabitants through to the apartheid years. *121 Bree St | admission free*

▶ Not only do you pay the lowest green fees in South Africa when you tee off at the Hans Merensky Golf Course, but you get to play in the company of wild game. It is next to the Kruger National Park and if a pride of lions happens to be heading that way, the course is closed. Five minutes from the Kruger's Phalaborwa Gate. *www.hansmerensky.com*

PRETORIA

(124 C4) *(J–K3)* **Overlooking Pretoria – now part of the Tshwane municipality (population of 4.7 million) – are the Union Buildings, built by the architect Sir Herbert Baker in 1910.**

It is from here that the country is governed, when Parliament is not in session in Cape Town. And it was here in the imposing building and amphitheatre that the inauguration of Nelson Mandela took place. The buildings are surrounded by a magnificent park that is bordered by the minister's residences and foreign embassies. In October the city transforms into a sea of purple when its 70,000 jacaranda trees burst into bloom.

SIGHTSEEING

NATIONAL ZOOLOGICAL GARDEN

This is known as one of the best in the world. A cable car will take you to viewing platforms so you get to see the enclosures and some of the 4340 different animals that live here. *Paul Kruger St | 8.30am–5.30pm | entrance fee 45 rand*

TRANSVAAL MUSEUM
Geological and archaeological finds and exhibits about prehistoric hominids. *Paul Kruger St | 9am–5pm daily | entrance fee 6 rand*

UNION BUILDINGS ★
Seat of government and architectural landmark on *Meintjieskop* where Nelson Mandela took his oath of office in 1994.

VOORTREKKER MONUMENT
The Voortrekkers built this memorial and museum in 1947 to commemorate their victory over the Zulu people at the Battle of Blood River in 1838. For conservative Afrikaners this has long been a symbol of their strength as a nation. *8am–4pm daily | entrance fee 50 rand*

FOOD & DRINK

JANICKY'S RESTAURANT
Traditional South African dishes like *pap en vleis* are served here. *165 Monroe St | tel. 0123 73 42 38 | Budget*

ZEMARA RESTAURANT
African and South African fusion cuisine with freshwater tilapia always on the menu. *Corner Park St/Wessel St | tel. 0123 44 15 26 | Moderate*

SHOPPING

INSIDER TIP THE YARD
If you prefer small alleys to shopping malls, then shops here will be just up your street. *Corner Duncan St/Prospect St*

CINNAMON LIFESTYLE & DESIGN
Perfect if you need a souvenir to take back to somebody who already has everything. *Shop 6, Monument Park, Shopping Centre, Skilpad Rd*

ENTERTAINMENT

CO.FI
Bar that is the 'in' meeting place, said to have the best DJs in town. Also has a restaurant. *Shop 1, Brooklyn Sq, corner Middle St and Veale St*

Pretoria as seen from the Union Buildings

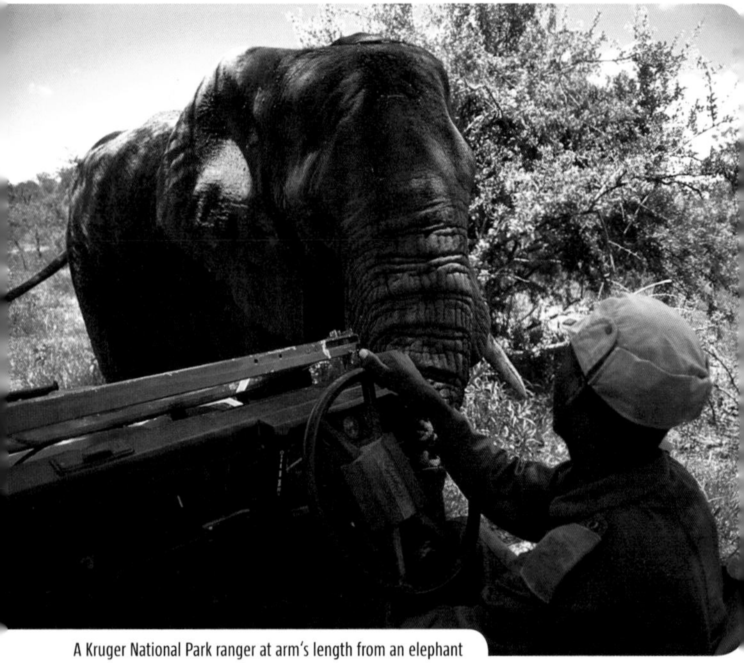

A Kruger National Park ranger at arm's length from an elephant

WHERE TO STAY

INSIDER TIP **ALPINE ATTITUDE HOTEL**
Stylish and chic boutique hotel with lots of art, each of the rooms has a theme like the *African Room* or the *Nature Room*. *10 rooms | 522 Atterbury Rd | www.alpineattitude.co.za |* Moderate

40 ON ILKEY
Comfortable B & B in the leafy suburb of Lynnwood in Pretoria. *7 rooms | 40 Ilkey Rd | Muckleneuk | tel. 0123483766 | www.40onilkey.co.za |* Budget

INFORMATION

TSHWANE TOURISM ASSOCIATION
309 Church Sq | tel. 0128412593 | www.tshwane.gov.za

WHERE TO GO

KRUGER NATIONAL PARK ★
(125 E–F 1–3) (*L–M 1–2*)
This 20,000km² (7722mi²) world famous game park is home to the most diverse number of animals on the African continent. Some 130 mammals, 48 fish, 114 reptile and 468 bird species live here. The park's inventory lists among others; 9000 elephants, 26,000 buffalos, 120,000 impalas as well as zebras, lions, leopards, giraffes, hippos and rhinos.
There are eight entry gates into the park. You can reach four of these from *Nelspruit* on the N4; *Malelane, Crocodile Bridge, Numbi* and the *Paul Kruger Gate*. Approximately halfway up the park there are the *Orpen* and *Phalabora* gates, while the *Punda Maria* and *Pafuri* gates are right

up in the north. The rest camps offer accommodation in rondavels or cottages. In the smaller camps you need to bring your own provisions, the bigger ones like *Pretoriuskop* and *Bergendahl* have restaurants and even swimming pools.
South Africa realised the need for nature conservation at an early stage. The Kruger National Park came about as a result of the government prohibiting hunting in the area between the Sabie and Crocodile Rivers way back in the 19th century.
The roads in the park are good and there is an extensive network of both surfaced and unsurfaced roads and tracks to explore. Visitors drive through in their own vehicles – ensure that doors and windows are shut at all times. The maximum speed on surfaced roads is 50km/h (31mi/h), on unsurfaced roads 40km/h (25mi/h) *(April–Oct 6am–6pm | Nov–March 5.30am–6.30pm | entrance fee 130 rand per person | information and reservations: Sanparks tel. 012 428 9111 | www.parks-sa.co.za)*. *220km (136mi) from Pretoria*

INSIDER TIP *The Outpost* on the border to neighbouring Zimbabwe and Mozambique is a private rest camp inside the Kruger National Park. The Makuleke tribe previously owned the land, were dispossessed of it when it became part of the park and then reclaimed it in the 1990s. The tribe received a concession for a private lodge to be built on the land. *The Outpost* offers 12 luxurious suites *(tel. 011 245 57 04 | www.theoutpost.co.za | Expensive)*.
If you prefer not to stay over in the Kruger National Park rest camps or at the more expensive private reserves then the *Graskop Hotel (40 rooms | tel. 013 767 12 44 | www.graskophotel.co.za | Budget)* in Graskop is a good option. Owner Harrie collects art and some of the hotel rooms are decorated with works by famous South African artists.

BOOKS & FILMS

▶ **Long Walk to Freedom** – In his autobiography Nelson Mandela gives a vivid account of his struggle against apartheid

▶ **Disgrace** – Nobel Literature Prize winner John M. Coetzee's novel was adapted into a film starring John Malkovich in 2007. A drama about a white father and daughter and their coming to terms with personal guilt and South Africa's past

▶ **Invictus** – Clint Eastwood directed this story, based on the famous Rugby World Cup final in 2009. It stars Matt Damon in the lead role with Morgan Freeman as Nelson Mandela

▶ **Red Dust** – This novel by Gillian Slovo (brought to the big screen by Tom Hooper in 2004) is about people from different backgrounds dealing with the Truth and Reconciliation Commission and its effects

▶ **Tsotsi** – South African production by director Gavin Hood that won an Oscar for the best foreign film in 2005. A moral tale of redemption in the townships, it is based on an adaptation of the award-winning Athol Fugard novel

▶ **Blood Safari** – Very gripping crime thriller by South African author, and international success story, Deon Meyer

LIMPOPO

(124–125 C–E 1–3) *(🗺 J–L 1–2)*

Despite its thriving agricultural sector, South Africa's Northern Province is the country's poorest. This is also as a result of large parts of it being a homeland under the apartheid government. The province remains relatively untouched by tourism but for a part of the Kruger National Park that falls under it. At the foot of the Klein Drakensberg lies the town of *Tzaneen* (population of 80,000). One theory on the origin of its name is that it is from the Khoikhoi language and means basket – referring to the fertile valley in which Tzaneen nestles. For accommodation head 15km (9.3mi) south to *Agatha* where you will find the small traditional hotel *The Coach House (45 rooms | Old Coach Rd | tel. 0153 06 80 00 | www.coachhouse.co.za | Moderate). 175km (108mi) from Pretoria*

MPUMALANGA

(125 D–E 3–4) *(🗺 K–L 2–4)*

This province is predominantly subtropical with fertile plains. On the *Panorama Route* you will have unparalleled views of typical African forests and savannah. The *Casa do Sol* hotel in *Hazeyview* is one of the best en route *(42 rooms | Sabie Rd | tel. 0137 37 81 11 | www.relaishotels.com | Moderate)*. A century or so ago gold (among other minerals) was discovered in *Barberton* but with the rapid depletion of the reserves it soon returned to being a sleepy little village.

You will find some of the country's most beautiful private game parks in this province, one of which is *Thornybush Game Reserve.* The best is *Royal Malewane,* stay at this game lodge and have top chef John Jackson spoil you. Every suite has its own small swimming pool. *10 rooms | on the road to Orpen Gate | tel. 0157 93 0150 | www.royalmalewane.com | Expensive*

Sabie is one of Mpumalanga larger cities. It is surrounded by dense forests and lots of waterfalls – the most well known is *Mac Mac Falls* 10km (6mi) away – and makes for a good starting point from which to set out to explore the scenic landscape of the *Blyde River Canyon*. The canyon is 15km (9.3mi) from Sabie via *Graskop.* Get the best view from *God's Window.*

Located only 5km (3mi) from Graskop is *Pilgrim's Rest,* a tiny village that is the product of South Africa's first gold rush. In 1873 Alex Patterson came across the first gold nuggets in a small tributary of the Blyde River while traversing the land with a wheelbarrow. He tried unsuccessfully to keep his discovery a secret, and in no time at all there was an influx of some 1500 prospectors. First they settled in tents but soon corrugated iron houses, shops and bars sprung up and one of them – the *Royal Hotel* – still exists today. Panning for gold came to an abrupt end after seven years and was replaced with underground mining when a company bought the mineral rights. The mine was finally shut down 100 years after that auspicious day when Patterson found his first nugget. Today *Pilgrim's Rest* is a listed outdoor museum. If you would like to try your luck then you too can also pan for gold. Find out more at the *Diggings Museum* at the town's entrance.

The entrance to *Mount Sheba Nature Reserve* is some 20km (12.4mi) from Pilgrim's Rest. The reserve does not have any big game; its main attraction is some 100 different tree species that are home to cavorting monkeys. The reserve is significant for its indigenous rain forest, making it a perfect ecosystem. Visitors wanting to explore the reserve on foot have a choice of 12 hiking trails ranging from 1000m to 6km (3.7mi). *Sheba's Look Out (6am–10pm daily | entrance fee*

15 rand) will give you the best views and *Forever Resort Mount Sheba (25 rooms | tel. 0124 23 56 00 | www.foreversa.co.za | Moderate)* is a good option for an overnight stay.

NORTH WEST PROVINCE

(124 A–C 3–5) (*F–J 2–4*)

This is a popular province as tourists come for its magnificent game reserves. One of the most well known is the INSIDER TIP *Pilanesberg Game Reserve* which is also easily accessible from Johannesburg, 110km (68mi) away. It is perfect for a brief getaway and an opportunity to see the *Big Five* in their natural habitat *(April–Aug 6am–6.30pm daily | Sept–March 5am–5pm daily | entrance fee 60 rand | an additional 20 rand vehicle charge)*.

Right in the north of North West Province is the INSIDER TIP *Madikwe Game Reserve*. This park has two huge advantages for the visitor. Firstly it is malaria-free and secondly it is never busy as it does not accept day visitors. You have to stay in one of their 30 private rest camps to see the reserve. One of the most beautiful is *Madikwe Safari Lodge* with its 20 thatched cottages nestled in the slope of the mountain with excellent views of the park and the animals *(tel. 0118 09 43 00 | www.andbeyondafrica.com | Expensive)*.

Curious impalas at Madikwe Game Reserve

TRIPS & TOURS

The tours are marked in green in the road atlas, pull-out map and on the back cover

1 WINE ROUTE OFF THE BEATEN TRACK

This is an interesting trip even if you are already familiar with the well known Cape wine estates. The drive begins in Franschhoek and takes you to Swellendam – via Villiersdorp, Worcester, Nuy and Robertson. A good idea is to set aside a whole day to do the 200km (124mi) stretch.

From South Africa's culinary capital **Franschhoek** → p. 58 head over the **Franschhoek Pass**. Once you have reached the highest point the road winds its way to the expansive **Theewaterskloof Dam**. It is partly surrounded by a game park (not fenced in). Now continue your journey to **Villiersdorp** where the wine lands begin again. All 80 farmers in this region belong to a cooperative and you can taste their wines at the **Kelkiewyn Farmstall**. The adjoining restaurant serves good home cooking. Meals served in lovely setting alongside the river *(Main Rd | tel. 02 88 40 09 00 | Budget)*.

Carry on along the R 43 to **Worcester**, surrounded by the country's biggest wine growing area that produces a fifth of the country's output. The **Kleinplasie Open Air Living Museum** just outside the town takes you back in time to the life of the

Photo: Namaqualand Daisies

Wild flowers, delicious wines and an untamed wilderness: discover South Africa by car, luxury train or bus

early pioneers and farmers. The buildings are reconstructions of houses in the Cape region *(Mon–Sat 9am–4.30pm | entrance fee 15 rand)*. Then there is the *KWV House of Brandy*, the country's main producer of brandy *(brandy tasting Mon–Fri 8.30am–4pm)*. Located very close to the N 1 is the **Aquila Safari Lodge**. Home to the Big Five it is just under two hours drive from Cape Town *(20 rooms | tel. 02 14 21 49 98 | www.aquilasafari.com | Moderate)*. Day visitors welcome.

Now take the R 60 in the direction of Robertson. After 15km (9.3mi) turn off left to **Nuy**. Aside from the exceptional wines produced here there is also the INSIDER TIP Nuy Valley Guest House with its somewhat eccentric touch: accommodation options include rooms in converted old wine tanks made of cement *(28 rooms |*

tel. 02 33 42 12 58 | www.nuyvallei.co.za | Budget).
A few kilometres further along the R 60 the **Robertson Valley** begins – a valley of wines and roses. The first cooperative you will come across is INSIDER TIP *Rooiberg* where you can purchase excellent wines at affordable prices. The town's top restaurant is *Bourbon Street (22 Voortrekker St | tel. 02 36 26 59 34 | Budget).*
From Robertson, continue another 15km (9.3mi) on the R 60, then turn right on to the R 312. Some excellent wine estates are located along this route e.g. **Bon Courage**, **De Wetshof**, **Van Loveren**, **Zandvliet** and especially **Springfield**, producers of one the region's best Chardonnay. Get back on to the R 60 in **Bonnievale** which connects up with the N 2 and to **Swellendam**, a charming historical town. It is the third oldest settlement in the Cape and dates back to 1745. One of the manor houses is home to the **Tourism Office** *(36 Voortrekker St | tel. 02 85 14 27 70)*. The open air **Drostdy Museum** *(Swellengrebel St | Mon–Sat 9am–4pm | entrance fee 20 rand)* is a showcase of buildings from the second half of the 18th century. The small *Augusta de Mist Country Estate (7 rooms | 3 Human St | tel. 02 85 41 24 25 | www.augustdemist.co.za | Moderate)* is highly recommended. Over the past two years the town has seen an influx of Belgians and they have brought with them their delectable cuisine in eateries like **La Belle Alliance** *(Swellengrebel St | tel. 02 85 14 22 52 | Budget).*

Excellent wines in the making

2 DRIVE THROUGH A SEA OF WILD FLOWERS

Millions of flowers bloom in the Western Cape from August to October, transforming the area in to a magnificent sea of colour. This floral show starts from around Darling and goes all the way to Springbok in the Namaqualand – and the most prolific are the Namaqualand daisies. It is 500km (310mi) from Cape Town to Vanrhynsdorp so it is best to allow for three days as there is plenty to see.
Take the N 7 north until you reach the Malmesbury exit. From there, head left to **Darling**. It is here that Pieter Dirk-Uys – renowned South African satirist, performer, author and social activist – has opened his own theatre in the old train station. During the apartheid era his alter-ego Evita Bezuidenhout would cleverly zero in on the political issues of the day. The theatre is called **Evita se Perron**, which translates as 'Evita's platform' *(tel. 02 24 92 39 30 | www.evita.co.za | Budget)*. The best B & B is **The Granary** *(6 rooms | 5 Long St | tel. 02 24 92 13 55 | www.thegranary.co.za | Budget).*

From Darling, take the R 307, then the R 45 to *Hopefield*. The small detour to the **West Coast Fossil Park** is well worth it *(Mon–Fri 9am–4pm, Sat/Sun 9am–noon | entrance 30 rand).* Between Hopefield and Velddrif is INSIDER TIP *Kersefontein* and one of the best options for a unique stay over in a Cape Dutch manor house that has been in the hands of one family, the Melcks, for 300 years *(7 rooms | tel. 02 27 83 08 50 | www.kersefontein.co.za | Moderate).*

Velddrif at the mouth of the Berg River on the Atlantic Ocean is in a spectacular setting and is a paradise for fisherman. If you prefer not to catch your own then try the seafood at *The Sunset (1 Garnaal St | tel. 02 27 83 27 63)* right on the beach. A visit to the **West Coast Gallery** not only showcases local artists but sells interesting products like *Khoisan bath crystals* made from salt with a high mineral content to relieve pain and to detox. The R 399 will take you back to the N 7. From there head further north and turn right on the R 364 in the direction **Clanwilliam**. Here in the Cedarberg is the country's centre for the production of rooibos tea and the only place in the world that the bush grows. For good food and reasonably priced accommodation try the **Clanwilliam Hotel** in the centre of town *(24 rooms | tel. 02 74 82 11 01 | www.clanwilliamhotel.co.za | Budget).*

To get to your next destination, instead of driving into Clanwilliam stay on the R 364 for another 36km (22.3mi). When you see the **Bushmans Kloof Wilderness Reserve** sign, it is only another 8km (4.9mi) until you get to this rather special hotel. It is a private game park at the foot of the Cedarberg Mountains that is home to 140 bird species and regional game (from the mountain zebra, to gemsbok to wildcats). It is also the site of more than 125 remarkable San rock paintings. They

African elephants – San rock art

depict animals and people and some are extremely well preserved. Since it is also a sanctuary and wellness retreat, be sure to indulge in some soothing pampering with a restorative Cederberg Soul'ution spa treatment. Enjoy an overnight stay at the **Bushmans-Kloof Wilderness Reserve & Retreat**. *(16 rooms | tel. 02 16 85 25 98 | www.bushmanskloof.co.za | Expensive).* Only natural products from the area are used.

From here the R 363 meets up with the R 27 and you take a left turn to **Nieuwoudtville**. From the **Bokkeveld Berg** plateau you can get a spectacular view of the flower splendour. Stay over at the **Van Zijl Guest Houses and Restaurant** *(10 rooms | tel. 02 72 18 15 35 | www.niewoudtville.co.za | Budget).* In **Vanrhynsdorp** you get back on to the N 7 either to Cape Town or to Namibia.

3 A CROSS COUNTRY LUXURY TRAIN RIDE

If you would like to travel in style through the Cape then a train trip with Rovos Rail is for you. If you do the Pretoria to Cape Town leg then you can look forward to 48 hours

of creature comforts as you travel the 1600km (994mi) through the breathtaking landscape of the Karoo.

Departure is on a Saturday afternoon from **Pretoria** → p. 88 station. The strains of a string quartet and a glass of champagne will await you in the impressive 1920 Sir Herbert Baker building. Then the historic locomotive, the *Pride of Africa* will roll out of the station on the first leg of the journey. The atmosphere is reminiscent of the Agatha Christie novel *Murder on the Orient Express*. There are two overnight options: the Royal Suites which are approximately 16m² (172ft²) in size and come with a double bed and private lounge area or the deluxe suites which are about 118ft² in size. The en suite bathrooms have all the modern conveniences and old world charm. Carriage no. 226, the observation and bar carriage, has been renovated and has enlarged windows for better viewing. Dinner is served at 8pm and the dress code is formal with a jacket and tie, the minimum requirement for men. The passenger numbers never exceed the number of people that can be seated in the dining carriage, a decisive feature that distinguishes it from the Blue Train with its two dinner sittings. The dishes are exclusive and served with select South African wines. Breakfast on the Sunday morning is served at 8am. At 10am the train pulls into **Kimberley** → p. 38 where passengers can join a sightseeing tour to the Big Hole, the Kimberley Mine Museum and the **Kimberley Club** – once the exclusive club for wealthy diamond barons. The next stretch is through 700km (435mi) of Karoo semi desert to the next stop. The Monday morning stop is at the historical town of **Matjiesfontein**. In 1876 a Scotsman by the name of Douglas Logan suffering from a lung disease discovered the healing properties of its climate and it remained a spa town for decades afterwards. The Matjiesfontein of today is virtually as it was then.

It takes the train another two hours before the landscape through which it winds changes dramatically. The dry Karoo makes way for the fertile Cape with its wine estates and orchards before you get your first glimpse of Table Mountain in the distance. The trip comes to an end in **Cape Town** → p. 49 at 6pm when the train pulls into the station *(prices and booking information p. 110)*.

4 BAZ BUS FROM JOHANNESBURG TO CAPE TOWN

Backpackers in South Africa get to travel and to stay cheaply, their best travel option is the Baz Bus *(tel. 02 14 39 23 23 | www.bazbus.com)*. You can do Johannesburg to Cape Town or the reverse and can get on and off as often as you wish (one way 3200 rand, return journey 4400 rand).

It is a good idea to book your backpacker hostels before you leave home. In Johan-

nesburg the **Shoestrings Airport Lodge** comes highly recommended. The owner Rob fetches his guests from the airport free of charge *(tel. 0119 75 04 74 | www.shoestringsafrica.com | Budget)*. Get your free copy of the backpacker bible *Coast to Coast* (which lists South Africa's best backpacker accommodation) at any of the backpacker hostels. The Baz Bus will often pick up passengers directly from their front door. Book your seat well in advance at peak times. The first leg of the journey is to the **Drakensberg** → p. 79 then on to Durban. If you decide to spend the night in Swaziland then go for **Swaziland Backpackers** *(Manzini | tel. 09269 5 28 20 38 | www.swazilandbackpackers.com)*. Staying over in **Durban** → p. 72 is an absolute must and a good overnight option is at **Banana Backpackers** *(61 Pine St | tel. 03 13 68 40 62 | www.bananabackpackers.co.za | Budget)*. For a small surcharge you can join the Baz Bus on a one of their city tours of Durban, Port Elizabeth or Cape Town. The route between Durban and Port Elizabeth has three of South Africa's most attractive backpacker hostels: The **Coffee Shack** directly on the beach in the isolated coastal town of **Coffee Bay** *(tel. 04 75 75 20 48 | www.coffeeshack.co.za | Budget)*; the **Buccaneers** in **Cintsa** with a breathtaking view of the Indian Ocean beaches *(tel. 04 37 34 30 12 | www.cintsa.com | Budget)*; and last but not least **Away with the Fairies** in **Hogsback** – a magical setting in a huge garden *(Bag End | Ambleside Close | tel. 04 59 62 10 31 | www.awaywiththefairies.co.za | Budget)*. An overnight stay in **Port Elizabeth** → p. 44 is mandatory because this is where the coach driver takes a break. The next stop is another must, **Jeffrey's Bay** → p. 47 and then in **Wilderness** stay over at the **Beach House Backpackers** *(Western Rd | tel. 04 48 77 05 49 | www.wildernessbeachhouse.com)*. From here it is only several more hours before you reach your destination, Cape Town. Here the Sunflower Stop Backpackers in Green Point is ideally located between the sea and the city *(Main Rd | tel. 02 14 34 65 35 | www.sunflowerstop.co.za)*. Just about all of the country's backpacker hostels are eco friendly.

Jeffrey's Bay beach – a popular holiday and surfing destination

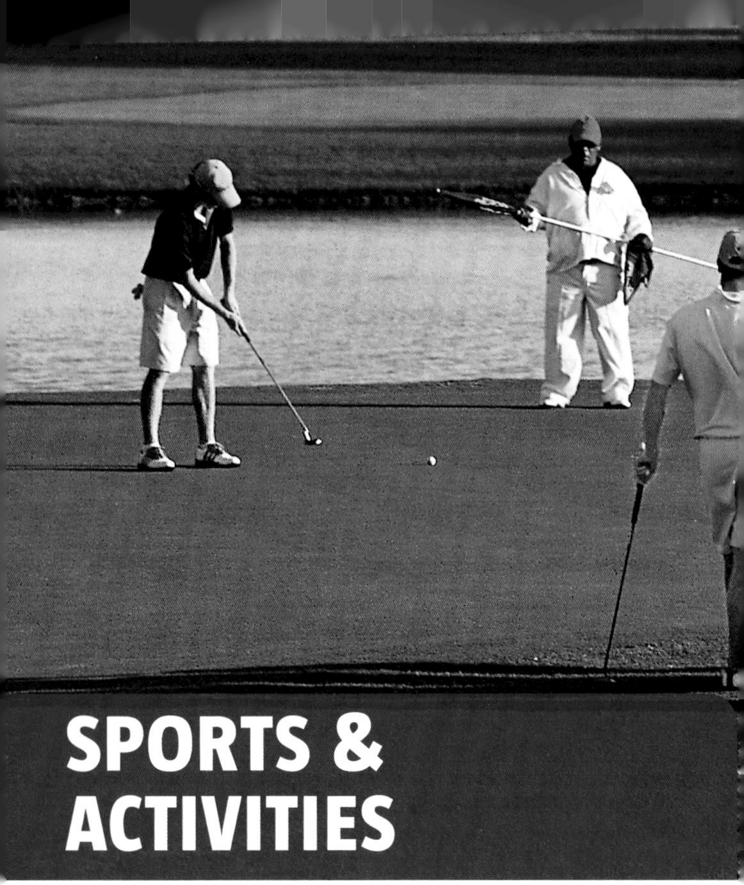

SPORTS & ACTIVITIES

Thanks to the country's wonderful climate locals enjoy an active, outdoor lifestyle and all sports are hugely popular. South Africa's hosting of the 2010 World Cup Soccer has come a long way in popularising the sport. Ranking second is rugby, with cricket third but regardless of what team is playing it will have the whole nation rooting for it!

BUNGEE JUMPING

Daredevils are invited to do the world's highest bungee jump, 216m (708ft) off the Bloukrans Bridge near Plettenberg Bay. *Tel. 04 22 81 14 58 | www.faceadrenalin.com*. If you are in Durban a great option is also from the Moses Mabhida Stadium.

CYCLING

Cycle lanes are not that common in South Africa so it is not a good idea to cycle in any of its cities. Cape Town is the exception as it has some dedicated lanes like the one between Hout Bay and the Waterfront. Hire a mountain bike from *Downhill Adventures (tel. 02 14 22 03 88)* and take part in a INSIDER TIP *Downhill Adventures Tour* down Table Mountain. It has some rather steep gradients but is well worth it for the crystal clear mountain pool you get to cool

Everything is possible in South Africa: a relaxing game of golf, an exciting shark dive or a ludicrously steep mountain bike cycle

off in at the halfway point. A cycling tour along the Garden Route is also an option *(info: African Bikers | tel. 02 14 65 20 18)*.

DEEP SEA DIVING

A particularly spectacular underwater landscape can be found in the sea at Plettenberg Bay. *Ocean Safaris (tel. 04 45 33 49 63 | www.oceansafaris.co.za)* rents out equipment. In Cape Town the best time for deep sea diving is between June and October, otherwise you may have a strong wind to contend with. Courses and equipment: *Table Bay Diving (tel. 02 14 19 88 22)*

GOLF

Golf remains an all-time favourite among locals and visitors alike. South Africa has

400 golf greens and many tournaments are played here. In the Kalahari the courses are drier than in those along the more tropical Indian Ocean. Bookings can generally be made at short notice except on Wednesday afternoons when enthusiasts tend to take the afternoon off for a round of golf. Green fees are negligible. *Golf in South Africa (www.golfinsouthafrica.com)* is the country's leading website for all the available resources and events. The most attractive golf resorts and hotels are: *Zimbali* north of Durban; *Fancourt* on the Garden Route and *Arabella Western Cape Hotel* outside of Cape Town *(145 rooms | tel. 02 82 84 00 00 | www.starwoodhotels.com | Expensive)*.

A unique experience is the INSIDER TIP *Hans Merensky Golf Course (www.hansmerensky.com)* in a nature reserve next to the Kruger National Park. There are very few places in the world where you get to tee off in the company of wild animals.

HANG-GLIDING

South Africa's mountainous terrain makes it perfect for this sport and you can hire the necessary equipment in Cape Town and KwaZulu-Natal. Ideal take-off spots are the Franschhoek Pass across the valley or Lion's Head across Cape Town's suburbs. The Drakensberg also has good options *(www.hanggliding.co.za)*.

HIKING

If peace and tranquillity are what you are after, hiking is a good bet. The five-day *Otter Trail* along the ocean in the *Tsitsikamma National Park* is one of South Africa's most popular. You need a permit for this hike and must you should book a year in advance! Information: *tel. 0124 28 9111 | reservations@parks-sa.co.za*

Entry to the *Franklin Game Reserve* is free of charge. It is located right in the middle of Bloemfontein and offers an en-

Ideal for thrill seekers – a shark dive

tirely different experience. En route up the steep hills with stunning views you may come across game such as springbok, gemsbok and wildebeest. The park is also home to three giraffes and many ostriches. Be alert as they can become a little aggressive. Information: *Bloemfontein Tourism | tel. 05 14 05 84 90*

HORSEBACK RIDING

One of the most beautiful places to go for a horseback ride is on the endless *Noordhoek* beach en route to Cape Point. *Sleepy Hollow Horseriding (tel. 02 17 89 23 41)* hires out horses.
The operator *Tswalu (www.tswalu.com)* takes visitors on horse safaris in the Kalahari desert. Riders can choose between a short hour-long ride or a day trip with picnic and siesta under the trees.

HOT-AIR BALLOONING

If it is a quiet adventure you are after then exploring the landscape from above is a great option. For 2300 rand *Bill Harrop's Original Balloon Safari (tel. 01 17 05 32 01 | www.balloon.co.za)* offers hot-air balloon rides over the Magaliesberg Mountains.

KITESURFING

Kitesurfing is the fastest growing water sport and the introduction of new and improved equipment makes it a little less dangerous than it once was. In Cape Town, the beach at Bloubergstrand or the Langebaan lagoon further up the West Coast are perfect for the sport. Kitesurfing is also popular in Port Elizabeth. Information: *www.safarinow.com or www.kite surfing.co.za.* In Durban there is only one outlet where you can hire equipment: *Ocean to Air* on the beach *(tel. 03 15 62 88 86 | www.oceantoair.com).*

MOTOR CYCLING

Born to be wild? If a high performance engine turns you on then why not hire a Harley and take a spin through the Cape peninsula. A good place to start is INSIDER TIP *Harley Davidson Tyger Valley (tel. 02 19 14 88 88 | www.hd-tygervalley.co.za)* which hires out the latest in bikes and also organises cross country tours. BMW fans will find their bike choice at *Karoo Biking (tel. 02 14 47 47 59).*

SHARK-CAGE DIVING

Always wanted to dive with the sharks? *White Shark Ecoventures* in *Gansbaai* (just over an hour's drive from Cape Town) will give you the opportunity to do so. For 1650 rand you can look right into the eyes of a great white from the safety of a cage. *Tel. 02 15 32 04 70 | www.white-shark-diving.com*

SURFING

South Africa is internationally known for its fantastic surf. *Jeffrey's Bay* on the Indian Ocean is *the* break of choice for the local and international pros who believe that the waves here are the best in the world *(Jeffrey's Bay Surf School | tel. 04 22 96 03 76)*. If you want to try your luck and are not afraid to test your skills in the icy waters of the Atlantic Ocean off Cape Town, find out more from *Downhill Adventures (tel. 02 14 22 03 88).*

WHITE WATER RAFTING

Although this sport is offered on many of the country's rivers the most exciting has to be the ride on the *Orange River* choose between a four or a six day trip *(information: Felix Unite | tel. 02 17 02 94 00 | www.felixunite.com).*

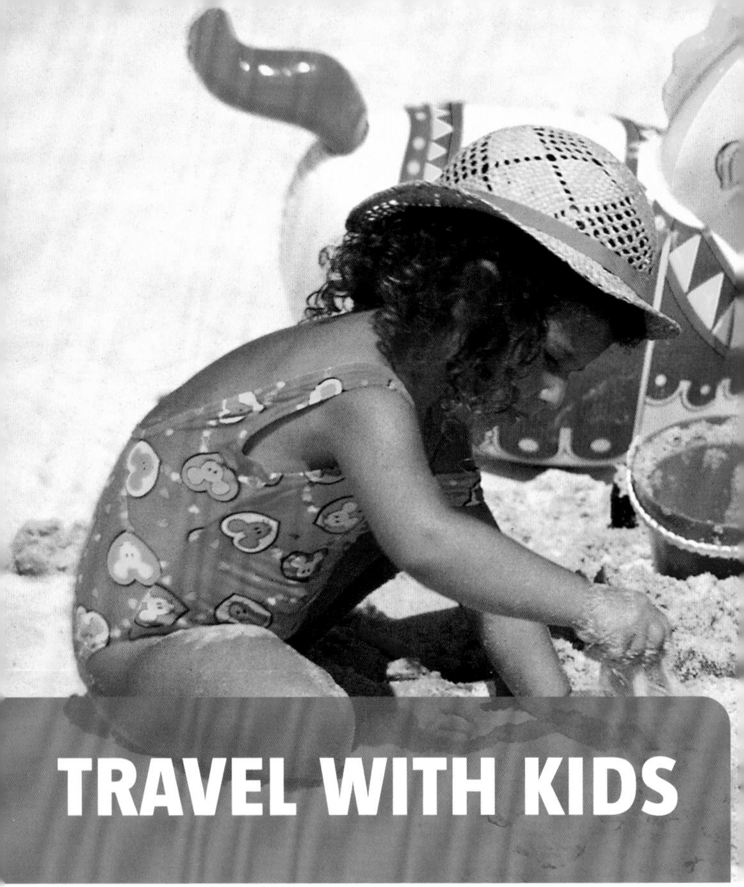

TRAVEL WITH KIDS

South Africa is a very child-friendly country and one that offers plenty of unique options like a hike to see San rock art, walking amongst penguins or feeding an ostrich.

Most restaurants have special children's menus, the waiters are generally very friendly to children and some restaurants even have crayons and colouring in books on hand. The larger hotels usually have a babysitter service and an events programme for children. To help set your mind at ease there are always lifeguards on duty at the popular beaches.

When making a family booking be aware of an increasing trend by small privately run guest houses and B & Bs to decline children (others will accept them but only from the ages of 12, 14 or 16). Even so, there is still ample accommodation specially designed with children in mind!

CAPE PROVINCES

BIRDS OF EDEN

(127 E6) (*🕮 G8*)

A top eco-tourism attraction on the Garden Route, this netted dome is the largest free flight bird aviary in the world and home to species from all the continents. *8am–5pm daily | adults 120 rand, children 60 rand | www.birdsofeden.co.za*

Amusement parks, game watching, boat rides: you will be spoilt for choice when it comes to fun things for the whole family to do

INSIDER TIP ELEPHANT SANCTUARY (127 E6) (*G8*)
An organization that provides young rescued elephants with a new lease on life until they are old enough to survive on a game reserve. Visitors learn everything about elephants and children even get to interact with them by touching and feeding them. *The Crags | Plettenberg Bay | tel. 04 45 34 81 45 | www.elephantsanctuary.co.za | adults 325 rand, children 175 rand*

INSIDER TIP KWANDWE PRIVATE GAME RESERVE (128 B5) (*J8*)
The Ecca Lodge camp, in this game park near Grahamstown, has rangers who are specially trained to instruct children. *6 rooms | tel. 0118 09 43 00 | www.kwandwereserve.co.za | Expensive*

OCEANS SAFARIS
(127 E6) (*G8*)
Boat trips from Plettenberg Bay to see whales, dolphins and seals up close. *From 12 years | adults 400 rand, children 200 rand | tel. 04 45 33 49 63*

CAPE TOWN & SURROUNDS

DUIKER ISLAND
(126 B6) (*D8*)
The glass-bottom boat, the *Calypso* sets out from Hout Bay, and it is the perfect way to see the seals on the island up close and personal! *42.50 rand per person | tel. 02 17 90 10 40*

MONKEY TOWN
(126 B5) (*D8*)
Spacious outdoor enclosures with over 20 species of primates. The monkeys, all born in captivity elsewhere and held in inappropriate conditions, were rescued and brought here by various animal rescue organisations. *Mondeor Rd | Somerset West | Cape Town | 9am–5pm daily | entrance fee 60 rand*

PLANETARIUM (U A4) (*a4*)
A special show takes children on a journey through the secrets of the universe where they get to see the world from a different perspective. *25 Queen Victoria St | Cape Town | tel. 02 14 81 39 00 | adults 25 rand, children 10 rand*

SCRATCH PATCH
(U F1–2) (*f1–2*)
Children get to sit in giant trays filled with hundreds of thousands of semi precious tumble-polished South African gemstones and 'scratch' for their favourites. The bags they fill are weighed and priced accordingly. *Diagonally opposite the Two Oceans Aquarium at the V&A Waterfront | daily 9am–6pm*

WIESENHOF GAME FARM
(126 B5) (*D8*)
A private game park with a picnic site, swimming pools, and a reserve with cheetah, zebra, ostrich and baboons. An ideal outing for children some 15km (9.3mi) from Cape Town. *Stellenbosch | on the R 44 at Klapmuts | tel. 02 18 75 51 81 | Tue–Sun 8am–6pm | entrance fee 28 rand*

WORLD OF BIRDS (126 B6) (*D8*)
Home to 3000 birds (also monkeys and reptiles) in spacious aviaries, visitors stroll through the aviaries on landscaped paths that are covered in wire. *Hout Bay | tel. 02 17 90 27 30 | 9am–5pm daily | adults 70 rand, children 40 rand*

KWAZULU-NATAL

INSIDER TIP **NATAL MARITIME MUSEUM** (129 E3) (*L5*)
Unusual museum made up of three actual ships, the young guests can explore them while learning about marine history and culture. *Beach Rd | Durban | Mon–Sat 8.30am–3.45pm, Sun 11am–3.45pm | admission free*

NORTHERN PROVINCES

FOOTLOOSE TROUT FARM
(124 C4) (*J3*)
Only children may fish for trout here and their catch can then be gutted for them. *Johannesburg | ask for directions when booking | tel. 01 14 66 99 11 | Tue–Fri 8am–5pm, Sat/Sun 7am–6pm | adults 50 rand, children 40 rand*

GOLD REEF CITY THEME & AMUSEMENT PARK (124 C4) (*K3*)
More than 20 terrific rides will have your children queuing for more but be sure they do not miss out on the best attraction of all; a trip down a 200m (656ft) deep

disused mine shaft where gold was once mined. *Johannesburg | M 1 south, Gold Reef City exit | tel. 0112486800 | 9.30am–5pm daily | entrance (from eight years upwards) 150 rand (inclusive of all the rides)*

JOHANNESBURG ZOO
(124 C4) (*⊞ J3*)

A very popular venue with lots of trees and beautiful walks. It has an impressive collection of over 3000 species (including the *Big Five*) and it is also home to Max, a gorilla famous for capturing a burglar who tried to escape via the ape enclosure. Offers a variety of educational programmes and is also open for night tours. *Forest Town | 8.30am–5.30pm daily | adults 50 rand, children 30 rand*

LIPIZZANER
(124 C4) (*⊞ J3*)

One of the few remaining spots in the world where Lipizzaner can be seen in action is here in Kyalami. Midway between Johannesburg and Pretoria. *Sun 10.30am | entrance (six years and over) 95 rand | tel. 0114682719*

INSIDER TIP VALLEY OF THE WAVES IN THE PALACE OF THE LOST CITY
(124 B3) (*⊞ J3*)

World class open air wave pool with slides catering for all ages! The water park has five rides, the most exciting of which is only for children. They do however have to be over 1.20m (3.9ft) in height. The rides have names like the Tarantula, the Mamba and the Scorpion. You can also float along a river through a jungle in a rubber dingy or play beach volleyball. There are also some botanical garden trails that lead through a variety of different forests. The greatest attraction of all: a simulated earthquake or volcanic eruption every hour. *Palace of the Lost City | 9am–6pm daily | adults 100 rand, children 50 rand*

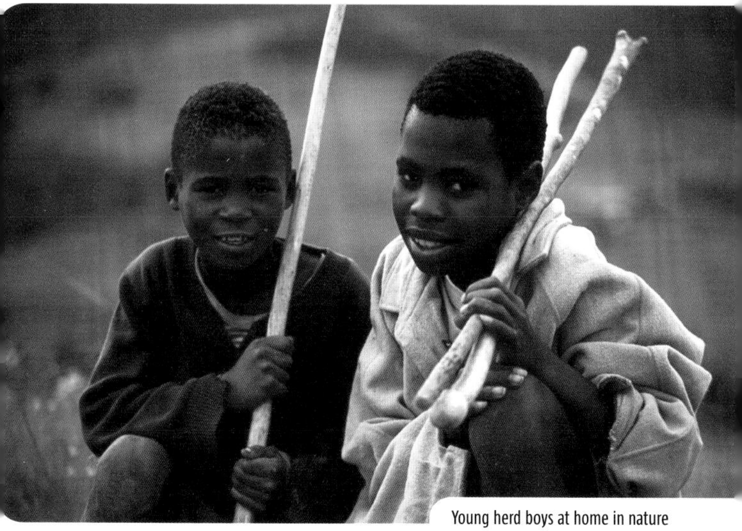

Young herd boys at home in nature

FESTIVALS & EVENTS

The traditional celebrations, festivals and events all reflect the wonderful diversity of the country's many and varied cultures.

PUBLIC HOLIDAYS

The following are public (bank) holidays when government offices, post offices, businesses but not necessarily all shops are closed: **1 Jan** *New Year's Day*; **21 March** *Human Rights Day*; **March/ April** *Good Friday, Easter Sunday, Family Day (Easter Monday)* **27 April** *Freedom Day*; **1 May** Workers' Day; **16 June** *Youth Day*; **9 Aug** *National Women's Day*; **24 Sept** *Heritage Day*; **16 Dec** *Day of Reconciliation*; **25 Dec** *Christmas Day* **26 Dec** *Day of Goodwill*. In the event of a public holiday falling on a Sunday the following Monday is a public holiday.

FESTIVALS & EVENTS

JANUARY

Cape Town: ▶ ***Cape Town Minstrel Carnival*** runs from 1st to 7th of January is staged by the city's ▶ ***coloured community:*** Performers from local communities dress in bright minstrel gear with parasols and dance and sing their way through the streets.

Cape Town: the country's most sophisticated and prestigious horse race the ▶ ***J & B Met*** is held at the ▶ ***Kenilworth Race Course*** on the last Sunday

MARCH

Oudtshoorn: ▶ ***Klein Karoo National Arts Festival*** a major cultural festival with theatrical productions and an art market in the last week of March

Cape Town: with 30,000 participants the ▶ ***Cape Argus Cycle Tour*** is the largest timed cycle event in the world, on the second Sunday in March

APRIL

Cape Town: national and international music buffs meet up for the ▶ ***Cape Town International Jazz Festival*** on the first weekend in April

JUNE

Pietermaritzburg and Durban: the gruelling annual ultra marathon, the ▶ ***Comrades Marathon***, is run between the two cities on the 16th June

Spectacular spring blossoms, music and dance: the vitality and variety of South Africa's festivals make them unique

JUNE/JULY
Grahamstown: ▶ ***National Arts Festival*** transforms the university town into an arts showcase for a fortnight from the last week in June to the first week in July

JULY
Knysna: the ▶ ***Knysna Oyster Festival*** where oysters are the focus for all the activities. Oyster-shucking and oyster eating competitions as well as sporting events. The first week in July
Franschhoek: ▶ ***Bastille Day festival*** on the Sunday closest to the 14th July. The wine estates, vintners and village restaurants get together to celebrate their French heritage with a wine and gourmet festival

AUGUST
Cape Town: held in the second week ▶ ***Cape Town Fashion Week*** showcases the country's designers

SEPTEMBER
Hermanus: held in the last week the ▶ ***Whale Festival*** celebrates the beautiful mammals that give birth in the bay between June and November

OCTOBER
Pretoria: massive ▶ ***Jacaranda Festival*** in the streets in the third week to pay tribute to the 70,000 trees that burst out in bloom
Stellenbosch: ▶ ***Food and Wine Festival*** showcases the area's wines starting on the last Wed through to Sat

DECEMBER
Sun City/Palace of the Lost City: the world's golfing greats are invited to the ▶ INSIDER TIP ***Sun City Million Dollar Challenge***

LINKS, BLOGS, APPS & MORE

LINKS

▶ www.sa-venues.com A site which will help you find accommodation even in the smallest town. Not necessarily all the establishments are listed but a small introduction is given to every town

▶ www.tripadvisor.com As is in many countries, the world's largest travel site, Tripadvisor is active here and provides tourists with reliable reviews and advice from real travellers. The destination experts in particular are well qualified

▶ www.zar.co.za Contains a wealth of information about South Africa with statistics, history, trivia and biographies of famous South Africans like Nelson Mandela

▶ www.whatidranklastnight.co.za Wine connoisseur Christian Eedes' blog tag line is: 'Good booze. Good food. Good company'. His blog combines wit and knowledge to report on his favourite wines and his favourite restaurants

▶ www.sprig.co.za An excellent blog that deals with all aspects of a sustainable and environmentally friendly South Africa. South Africa fast catching up when it comes to renewable energy sources

▶ www.groupon.co.za A site that offers an endless range of daily specials from hotel and B&B accommodation, spa treatments and adventure sports at a fraction of the price. It is easy to join and an absolute must before you plan your trip to South Africa

VIDEOS

▶ www.southafrica.info/video Worth checking out for the amazing travel videos that it showcases. Some also touch on the socio-political issues from an insider's view

Regardless of whether you are still preparing your trip or already in South Africa: these addresses will provide you with more information, videos and networks to make your holiday even more enjoyable

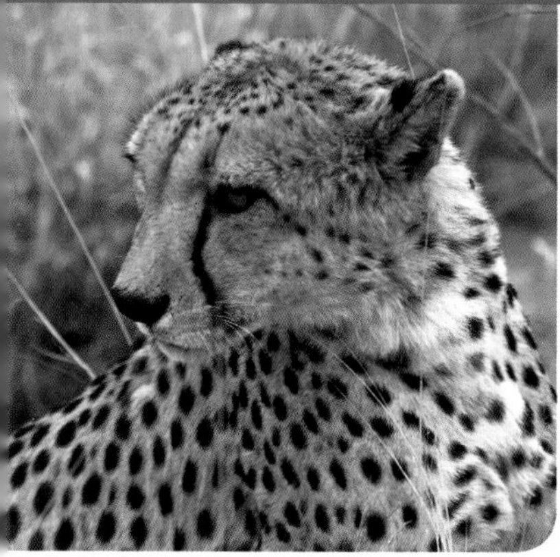

VIDEOS & STREAMS

▶ www.myvideo.co.za Anyone can post their mobile phone videos here. A colourful mix of topics on all aspects of life in South Africa

▶ www.africam.com/wildlife A site where you can watch safari destinations via live cams. In some game parks the camera is on the watering holes. Almost as good as being there

APPS

▶ John Platter Wine Guide The bible of South African wines and you can now load the app on to your mobile phone. Makes choosing the right wine a whole lot easier and more fun

▶ Food 24 A feast for foodies! Information on more than 3000 restaurants at your finger tips, with reviews by patrons and price comparisons. Free of charge

▶ CoPilot South Africa The best satnav system for South Africa can be bought for a little as 300 rand. Be aware though that many of the unpopulated stretches do not appear on the system

NETWORK

▶ www.facebook.com/MySouthAfrica Follows the South African Tourism board on Facebook. Lots of news, travel information and tips from fellow travellers.

▶ twitter.com/#!/gotosouthafrica The official twitter account for South African Tourism with tweets about cultural events, specials and some beautiful photographs

▶ www.airbnb.com Airbnb Is the popular site for travellers who prefer to stay in private accommodation offered by locals. A search for example under Cape Town pulls ups the full spectrum from a room in a private home through to a luxury villa that was once an embassy. The site is constantly updated with new listings and user reviews.

TRAVEL TIPS

ARRIVAL

O. R. Tambo International Airport outside Johannesburg is the major arrival point for international travellers. Most countries now offer regular direct flights to O. R. Tambo as well as to Cape Town International Airport. *South African Airways (www.flysaa.com)* has regular scheduled flights from major international cities. Some airlines regularly offer specials so it is worth taking a look other airlines like *British Airways (www.britishairways.com)* and *Emirates (www.emirates.com)*. The cheapest fares are in winter from April to September, the most popular (and expensive) are in summer from December to May. Book well in advance to avoid disappointment. Aside from SAA there are several other domestic airlines like *South African Airlink (www.saairlink.co.za)* and *South African Express (www.saexpress.co.za)* for flights inside South Africa.

RESPONSIBLE TRAVEL

It doesn't take a lot to be environmentally friendly whilst travelling. Don't just think about your carbon footprint whilst flying to and from your holiday destination but also about how you can protect nature and culture abroad. As a tourist it is especially important to respect nature, look out for local products, cycle instead of driving, save water and much more. If you would like to find out more about eco-tourism please visit: *www.ecotourism.org*

CAMPING

Its moderate climate makes South Africa an ideal destination for campers. Camping sites are found in all cities, on many beaches, in nature reserves and in conservation areas *(information tel. 03 33 26 13 70 | www.caravanparks.co.za)*. You can hire a camper van from rental companies like *Around About Car (www.aroundaboutcar.com)*.

CAR HIRE

The minimum age to hire a car is 23. An international driver's licence is a prerequisite. In peak season a medium range car with a 200km (124mi) daily mileage limit will cost you in the region of 2500 rand for a fortnight. Main outlets: *Avis (www.avis.co.za)*, *Budget (www.budget.co.za)* or *Hertz (www.hertz.co.za)*.

CONSULATES & EMBASSIES

BRITISH EMBASSY IN PRETORIA

255 Hill Street | Arcadia 0002 | Tshwane (Pretoria) | tel. 02 71 24 21 75 00 | ukinsouthafrica.fco.gov.uk

BRITISH CONSULATE GENERAL IN CAPE TOWN

Southern Life Centre | 15th Floor | 8 Riebeeck Street | Cape Town 8001 | tel. 02 14 05 24 00

CANADIAN EMBASSY IN PRETORIA

1103 Arcadia Street | Tshwane (Pretoria) | tel. 02 71 24 22 30 00 | www.canadainternational.gc.ca/southafrica-afriquedusud

CANADIAN CONSULATE CAPE TOWN

5 De Lorentz Street | Gardens | Cape Town | tel. 02 72 14 23 52 40

From arrival to weather

Holiday from start to finish: the most important addresses and information for your trip to South Africa

U.S. EMBASSY IN PRETORIA
877 Pretorius Street | Tshwane (Pretoria) | tel. 012 431 40 00 | southafrica.usembassy.gov

U.S. CONSULATE GENERAL CAPE TOWN
2 Reddam Ave | Westlake 7945 | tel. 02 72 17 02 73 00 | southafrica.usembassy.gov/consulate_capetown.html

The Zulu people make up South Africa's biggest population group

CUSTOMS

Among others the following goods can be imported duty-free to South Africa: 1 L spirits, 200 cigarettes and goods not exceeding 200 rand in value. The following goods can be imported duty-free into the EU: 1 L spirits, 200 cigarettes and goods not exceeding 390 pounds in value. Do not take a risk by exporting protected plant and animal species or their products. It is strictly prohibited by law. By the same token the importation of seeds and plants is also not permitted. For more information go to http://*south-africa.visahq.com/customs*

DRIVING

Third party insurance to cover passenger and motor vehicle liability is compulsory for anyone driving a vehicle in South Africa. Car rental companies include this in their rates. The speed limit in towns and cities is 60km/h, on provincial routes 100km/h and on the motorway 120km/h. Fines for speeding can be exorbitant. You drive on the left hand side of the road.
Around 84,000km of road is surfaced, another 163,000km is not. Some motorways are toll roads, like the one that links Johannesburg and Durban and almost the entire distance from Johannesburg to the Kruger National Park. These routes are demarcated with a white T on a blue background and you can pay by credit card. The South African traffic rules governing a four-way stop can be confusing for tourists. Whoever arrives at the intersection first drives off first. The other cars follow along the same principle. The Automobile Association of South Africa (AA) is represented throughout the country.

ELECTRICITY

220 Volt/50 cycles per second. Three pronged plugs are the norm so you may require an adapter. Hotels will generally be able to provide one.

EMERGENCY SERVICES

For a police emergency 10111 | ambulance and fire brigade 10177 | emergency number from a mobile phone 122 | tourist crisis incident reporting 08 61 87 49 11

HEALTH

Visitors to the Kruger National Park and to the Limpopo, Mpumalanga and KwaZulu-Natal nature reserves and adjoining areas are advised to take malaria prophylaxis. You can buy malaria tablets without a script in any chemist in the country and need only start the course on arrival in South Africa. No inoculations needed. Found in all the cities and larger towns, South Africa's privately run hospitals are state-of-the-art and their healthcare world class. NHS or government health insurance certificates from other countries are not accepted here. It is imperative that you take out appropriate travel insurance.

CURRENCY CONVERTER

£	ZAR	ZAR	£
1	12	10	0.80
3	36	30	2.50
5	60	50	4.20
13	156	130	11
40	480	400	33
75	900	750	62.50
120	1440	1200	100
250	3000	2500	208
500	6000	5000	417

$	ZAR	ZAR	$
1	7.50	10	1.30
3	23	30	3.90
5	38	50	6.50
13	100	130	17
40	300	400	50
75	550	750	97
120	900	1200	155
250	1850	2500	325
500	3700	5000	650

For current exchange rates see www.xe.com

IMMIGRATION

Visitors entering South Africa must be in possession of a valid passport and visitors from the UK, EU, USA, Australia and New Zealand do not require a visa for a stay of 90 days or less. Passports must be valid for six months and should have at least two unused pages.

INFORMATION

SOUTH AFRICAN TOURISM UK
6 Alt Grove London SW19 4DZ. Call centre 0870 1550 044 | www.southafrica.net/sat/content/en/uk/uk-home

SOUTH AFRICAN TOURISM USA
500 5th Avenue 20th Floor, Suite 2040, New York NY 10110. Call centre 1 800 593 1318 | www.southafrica.net/sat/content/en/us/us-home

GENERAL INFORMATION: *www.southafrica.info* and *www.sa-venues.com*

ADDITIONAL INFORMATION: accommodation: *www.portfoliocollection.com;* events bookings: *www.computicket.com;* game parks: *www.sanparks.org.*

INTERNET

There are Internet cafes in all towns and cities and airports and many hotels have Wi-Fi access.

MONEY, BANKS & CREDIT CARDS

The currency is the rand. It can be up to 20 per cent cheaper to exchange money in South Africa itself. Most banks will exchange travellers' cheques. You can withdraw cash using your Visa, MasterCard or debit card at most ATMs. Bank opening times: Mon–Fri 9am–3.30pm, Sat 9am–11am. All credit cards are accepted. Petrol stations should accept credit cards but best to check before you fill up, which incidentally is not self-service as all stations employ service attendants to fill your vehicle.

OPENING TIMES

Stores in South Africa are generally open from Monday to Friday 8.30am to 5pm and 9.30am to 1pm on Saturdays. Some larger shopping centres are open seven days a week until 8pm or 5pm on Saturdays and 1pm Sundays. The V & A Waterfront in Cape Town is open 365 days a year from 10am to 9pm.

POST

Opening times: *Mon–Fri 8.30am–4.30pm, Sat 8am–noon.*

PHONE & MOBILE PHONE

You will always dial ten digits to make a call locally; land line numbers all include the city code. You can hire a mobile phone at the airport on arrival or bring your own if you have confirmed with your service provider that it is compatible. Using your credit card you can hire a SIM card on arrival for around 20 rand a day and 5 rand per minute. Alternatively buy a starter pack from any cell phone service provider store: *Cell C (www.cellc.co.za), MTN (www.mtn.co.za), Vodacom (www.vodacom.co.za)*. Prepaid air time is sold at supermarkets, malls or petrol stations. You will need to show your passport and airline ticket.

The code for phoning overseas from South Africa is 00 followed by the country code, e.g. UK 0044, USA and Canada 001, Australia 0061. The code for calling South Africa is 0027.

BUDGETING

Kruger Nat. Park	192 rand *entrance fee per person*
Filter coffee	10 rand *per cup*
Coca Cola	6.50 rand *per standard can*
Newspaper	12 rand *for a national daily*
Sunscreen	approx. 50 rand *a tube*
Rump steak	120 rand *for 300 g in a restaurant*

Important phone numbers: *10 23 local information | 109 03 international information*

PRIVATE ACCOMMODATION

BACKPACKER HOSTELS

Accommodation options for backpackers in South Africa are excellent. Many hostels offer double rooms with private bathrooms in addition to dormitories. They are even good option for tourists travelling with a suitcase – considerably cheaper than a B & B. Get your free copy of the backpacker bible, *Coast to Coast* from any backpacker hostel *(www.coasttocoast.co.za).*

BED & BREAKFAST

There is no shortage of Bed & Breakfast accommodation in South Africa. Often their owners are also well versed in assisting their guests with travel enquiries. For listings of top class B & Bs get the *Portfolio Collection* catalogue from any travel agency. *Central reservations tel. 02 16 89 40 42 | www.portfoliocollection.com*

PUBLIC TRANSPORT

The transport systems in the cities hosting the 2010 World Cup Soccer benefited greatly from the event.

BUS

MyCiTi is Cape Town's new rapid bus service which includes a shuttle service between Cape Town International Airport and central Cape Town.

MINIBUS

The minibus taxi carrying up to 15 passengers is the means of transport most frequented by the locals. They do specific routes, service all areas and will stop anywhere on request.

RAIL

Gautrain is the new 80km (50mi) rapid transit railway system linking Johannesburg, Pretoria and O.R. Tambo International Airport. *For information on routes, prices and stations go to www.gautrain.co.za*

Taking a regular train between tourist destinations is not recommended. They are often slow and uncomfortable, which is why most holidaymakers make use of luxury trains.

Take the *Blue Train* between Cape Town and Pretoria and the journey with only one stop will take you as little as 24 hours. The train departs on a Monday, Wednesday and Friday in both directions. A one way ticket costs between 10,930 rand and 18,750 rand per person depending on the time of year and whether you share a compartment. *Reservations tel. 012 334 84 59 | www.bluetrain.co.za*.

The golden age of the steam train is still alive and well on the first leg of the journey with *Rovos Rail.* A single trip within

WEATHER IN JOHANNESBURG

	Jan	Feb	March	April	May	June	July	Aug	Sept	Oct	Nov	Dec
Daytime temperatures in °C/°F	26/79	25/77	24/75	22/72	19/66	17/63	17/63	20/68	23/73	25/77	25/77	26/79
Nighttime temperatures in °C/°F	15/59	14/57	13/55	10/50	6/43	4/39	4/39	6/43	9/48	12/54	13/55	14/57
Sunshine hours/day	8	8	7	8	9	9	9	10	9	9	9	9
Precipitation days/month	13	9	8	7	3	1	0	1	2	8	11	12

Durban surfers in search of the perfect wave

South Africa costs between 12,000 and 24,000 rand per person *(tel. 012 315 82 42 | www.rovosrail.com)*.
Rovos Rail mainly differs from the Blue Train in that it takes twice as long: 48 hours. It is a more relaxed way to travel, the slower speeds allow you to open a window and it stops at tourist spots. At night the train remains stationary for a few hours to let passengers sleep more peacefully.

SAFARI

There are game reserves for every taste and budget. The state-run game reserves are good value for money but are best booked a year in advance: *National Parks (tel. 012 428 9111 | reservations@parks.sa.co.za)*. KwaZulu-Natal administers the state-run nature reserves within its borders separately to the aforementioned *(tel. 033 845 10 02 | www.rhino.org.za)*. The best time to visit a game reserve is during the South African winter (April to September). In the rainy summer season the game is not drawn to the best observation spots, the watering holes. The lush vegetation also means less visibility. NB: Always keep your car windows closed, stay on the designated roads and do not get out of your vehicle.

TAX REFUND

You are eligible to be refunded 14 per cent VAT on a purchase of 250 rand or more, provided you can present a tax invoice. Refunds at the airport and in Cape Town also at *Waterfront Tourism*.

TIME

South Africa is on Central African Time (CAT) which is one hour ahead of the UK during the South African summer and two hours during the South African winter.

TIPPING

It is common practice to leave a tip of between 10 und 15 per cent of the total. This is especially the case in restaurants. In South Africa your bill does not include the waiter's gratuity – at least in most cases. In the larger cities and tourist area some restaurants now add a 10 per cent service charge on to the bill so it is a good idea is to read the small print.

NOTES

ROAD ATLAS

The green line ▬ indicates the Trips & tours (p. 94–99)
The blue line ▬ indicates the Perfect route (p. 30–31)

All tours are also marked on the pull-out map

Photo: Forest of quiver trees

Exploring South Africa

The map on the back cover shows how the area has been sub-divided

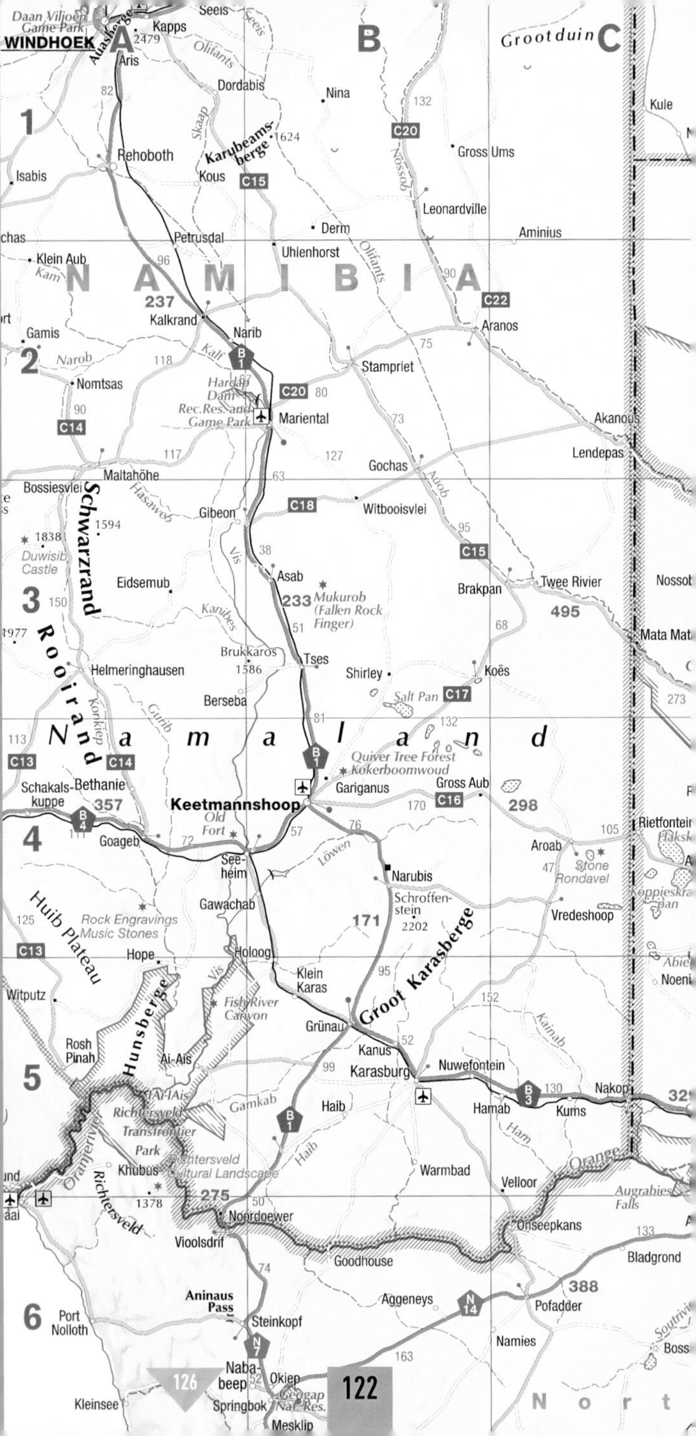

Daan Viljoen Game Park
WINDHOEK
Auasberge
Seeis
Kapps
2479
Aris
A
B
C
Grootduin
Olifants
Dordabis
Nina
Kule
1
82
Skaap
Karubeams-berge
1624
132
C20
Gross Ums
Nossob
Rehoboth
Isabis
Kous
C15
Leonardville
Derm
Aminius
chas
Petrusdal
Uhlenhorst
Klein Aub
Kam
96
Olifants
90
N A M I B I A
C22
237
Kalkrand
Narib
Aranos
Gamis
2
Narob
118
Kalf
B1
75
Stampriet
Nomtsas
Hardap Dam Rec.Res. and Game Park
C20
80
90
Mariental
C14
73
Akanous
117
127
Lendepas
Maltahöhe
63
Gochas
Bossiesvlei
Schwarzrand
Hasawes
Auob
C18
Witbooisvlei
Gibeon
1594
1838
Duwisib Castle
38
95
C15
Vis
Asab
Eidsemub
Mukurob (Fallen Rock Finger)
Brakpan
Twee Rivier
Nossob
3
150
233
495
Kanibes
51
68
1977
Rooirand
Mata Mata
Brukkaros
1586
Tses
Helmeringhausen
Shirley
Koës
Berseba
Salt Pan
C17
Konkiep
Gurib
81
132
113
N a m a l a n d
C13
C14
B1
Quiver Tree Forest
Kokerboomwoud
Schakals-kuppe
Bethanie
Gariganus
Gross Aub
357
Keetmannshoop
170
C16
298
B4
Old Fort
76
105
Rietfontein
4
Goageb
72
57
Aroab
Löwen
See-heim
Narubis
47
Stone Rondavel
Koppieskraal pan
Huib Plateau
Schroffen-stein
Gawachab
2202
Vredeshoop
125
Rock Engravings
Music Stones
171
Groot Karasberge
C13
Hope
Holoog
Abiel
Noeni
Vis
95
Klein Karas
Witputz
Fish River Canyon
152
Hunsberge
Kainab
Grünau
Rosh Pinah
Kanus
52
Ai-Ais
99
Nuwefontein
5
Karasburg
B3
130
Nakop
Ai-Ais Richtersveld Transfrontier Park
Gamkab
Haib
Hamab
Kums
B1
Ham
Richtersveld Cultural Landscape
Haib
Khubus
Warmbad
Orange
Oranjerivier
Velloor
275
Augrabies Falls
1378
50
Richtersveld
Noordoewer
Onseepkans
133
Vioolsdrif
Goodhouse
Bladgrond
74
388
Aninaus Pass
Aggeneys
N14
Pofadder
6
Port Nolloth
Steinkopf
Namies
N7
163
Soutrivier
Boss
126
Naba-beep
52
Okiep
Geogap Nat. Res.
Kleinsee
Springbok
Mesklip
N o r t

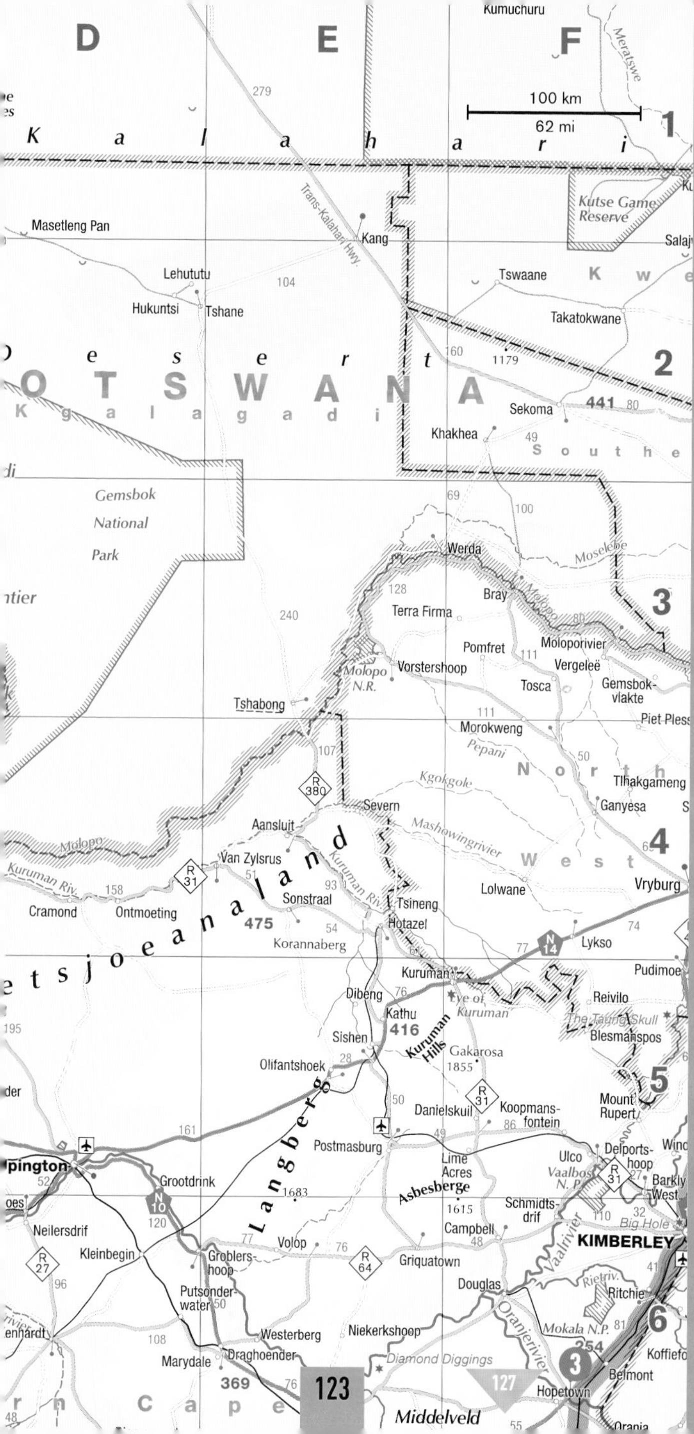

D E F

Kumuchuru

Meratswe

1

100 km
62 mi

Kutse Game
Reserve

Ku

Salaj

K a l a h a r i

279

Masetleng Pan

Trans-Kalahari Hwy.

Kang

Lehututu

104

Tswaane

K w e

Hukuntsi Tshane

Takatokwane

2

O E S E R T

O T S W A N A

160 1179

Sekoma **441** 80

K g a l a g a d i

Khakhea

49

S o u t h e

Gemsbok

National

69 100

Park

Werda

Moselebe

240

128

Terra Firma Bray

3

ntier

Molopo

Pomfret Moloporivier

Molopo
N.R.

Vorstershoop

111 Vergeleë

Gemsbok-
vlakte

Tshabong

Tosca

Piet Pless

107

111

Morokweng

Pepani

Kgokgole

50

Tlhakgameng

N o r t h

Severn

Mashowirivier

Ganyesa

S

Aansluit

Kuruman Rw.

4

R
380

W e s t

R
31

Van Zylsrus

93

Lolwane

Vryburg

Mulopo

51 Sonstraal

54

Tsineng

74

Kuruman Riv.

158

475

Hotazel

Cramond Ontmoeting

Korannaberg

77 N
14

Lykso

195

Dibeng

76

Pudimoe

etsjoeanaland

Kathu

*Eye of
Kuruman*

Reivilo

Kuruman

The Tswalu Skull

Sishen

Blesmanspos

Olifantshoek

28

Kuruman
Hills

Gakarosa
1855

5

R
31

161

50

Danielskuil

Koopmans-
fontein

86

Mount
Rupert

Postmasburg

49

Ulco

Delports-
hoop

Wind

Langberg

pington

Grootdrink

Lime
Acres

Vaalbos
N.P.

R
31

Barkly
West

N
10

120

52

1683

Asbesberge

Schmidts-
drif

110

32

Big Hole

oes

Neilersdrif

Volop

76

1615

Campbell

48

KIMBERLEY

R
27

Kleinbegin

Groblers-
hoop

77

R
64

Griquatown

Rietriv.

41

96

Putsonder-
water

50

Douglas

Ritchie

6

enhardt

108

Westerberg

Niekerkshoop

Mokala N.P. **354**

81

Koffiefo

Marydale

Draghoender

Diamond Diggings

3

Hopetown

Belmont

369

123

127

Middelveld

55

Orania

n C a p e

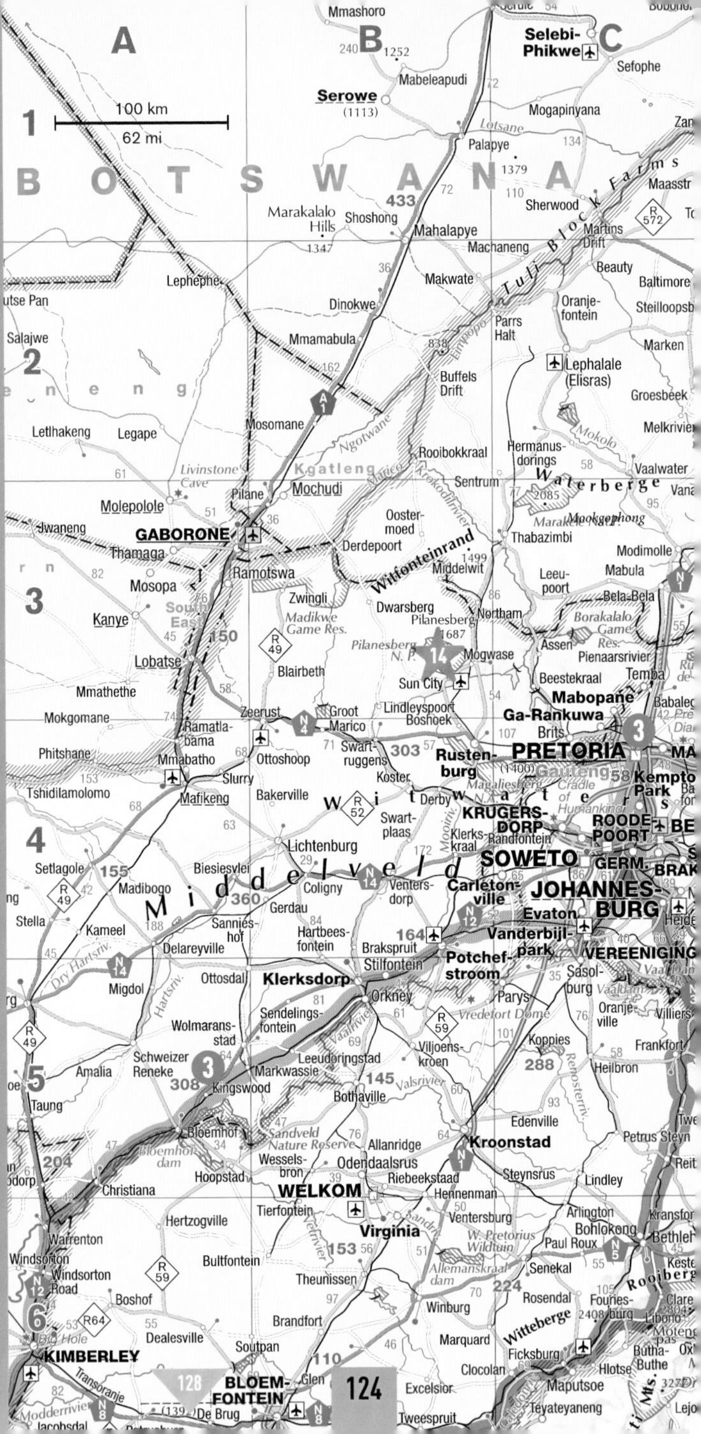

A
B
C
1
2
3
4
5
6
100 km
62 mi
BOTSWANA
Mmashoro
Selebi-Phikwe
Sefophe
Mabeleapudi
Serowe
(1113)
Mogapinyana
Lotsane
Palapye
1379
Sherwood
Tuli Block Farms
Maasstr
R 572
Marakalalo Hills
1347
Shoshong
433
Mahalapye
Machaneng
Martins Drift
Beauty
Baltimore
Makwate
Lephephe
Dinokwe
Oranje-fontein
Steilloopsb
Parrs Halt
Salajwe
Mmamabula
Marken
838
Limpopo
Lephalale (Elisras)
Buffels Drift
Groesbeek
A1
Mosomane
Ngotwane
Mokolo
Melkrivier
Letlhakeng
Legape
Rooibokkraal
Hermanus-dorings
Vaalwater
Livinstone's Cave
Kgatleng
Marico
Krokodilrivier
Sentrum
Waterberge
2085
Molepolole
Pilane
Mochudi
Oostermoed
Marakele Nat. P.
Mookgophong
Jwaneng
GABORONE
Thabazimbi
Thamaga
Derdepoort
Witfonteinrand
1499
Modimolle
Mabula
Middelwit
Leeu-poort
Ramotswa
Mosopa
Zwingli
Bela-Bela
N1
Kanye
South East
150
Madikwe Game Res.
Dwarsberg
Pilanesberg
Northam
Borakalalo Game Res.
1687
R 49
Pilanesberg N.P.
14
Mogwase
Assen
Pienaarsrivier
Lobatse
Blairbeth
Sun City
Beestekraal
Temba
Mmathethe
Mabopane
Babaleg
Mokgomane
Zeerust
Groot Marico
Lindleyspoort
Boshoek
Ga-Rankuwa
Brits
Ramatla-bama
N4
Swart-ruggens
303
Rustenburg
PRETORIA
3
Phitshane
Mmabatho
Ottoshoop
(1400)
Gauteng
Kempton Park
Tshidilamolomo
Slurry
Koster
Magaliesberg
Cradle of Humankind
Mafikeng
Bakerville
Witwatersrand
R 52
Derby
KRUGERS-DORP
ROODE-POORT
Swart-plaas
Mooiriv.
Klerks-kraal
Randfontein
Lichtenburg
SOWETO
GERM.
BRAK
Setlagole
155
Biesiesvlei
Middelveld
Coligny
N14
Venters-dorp
Carleton-ville
JOHANNES-BURG
Madibogo
360
Gerdau
Evaton
R 49
N12
Stella
Kameel
Sannies-hof
Hartbees-fontein
164
Vanderbijl-park
Dry Hartsriv.
Delareyville
Brakspruit
Stilfontein
Potchef-stroom
VEREENIGING
N14
Ottosdal
Klerksdorp
Sasol-burg
Vaaldam
Migdol
Hartsriv.
Orkney
Parys
R 49
Wolmarans-stad
Sendelings-fontein
Vaalrivier
R 59
Vredefort Dome
Oranje-ville
Villiers
Koppies
Frankfort
Schweizer Reneke
Leeudoringstad
Viljoens-kroen
288
Heilbron
Amalia
3
Markwassie
Renosterriv.
308
Kingswood
145
Valsrivier
Taung
Bothaville
Edenville
Bloemhof
Sandveld Nature Reserve
Allanridge
Kroonstad
Petrus Steyn
204
Bloemhof dam
Wessels-bron
Odendaalsrus
N1
Steynsrus
Christiana
Hoopstad
Riebeekstaad
Lindley
WELKOM
Hennenman
Tierfontein
Ventersburg
Arlington
Kransfor
Hertzogville
Virginia
Sandriv.
W. Pretorius Wildtuin
Bohlokong
Warrenton
Vetrivier
153
Paul Roux
Bethleh
Windsorton
N5
Bultfontein
Allemanskraal dam
Senekal
Windsorton Road
R 59
Theunissen
224
Rooiberg
N12
Boshof
Rosendal
Fouries-burg
Clare
2408
Winburg
Witteberge
Libono
Motena pas
R64
Brandfort
Big Hole
Dealesville
Marquard
Ficksburg
Butha-Buthe
KIMBERLEY
Soutpan
110
Hlotse
Clocolan
Transoranje
128
BLOEM-FONTEIN
Glen
Excelsior
Maputsoe
Modderrivier
N8
(1394)
De Brug
N8
Tweespruit
Teyateyaneng
Jacobsdal

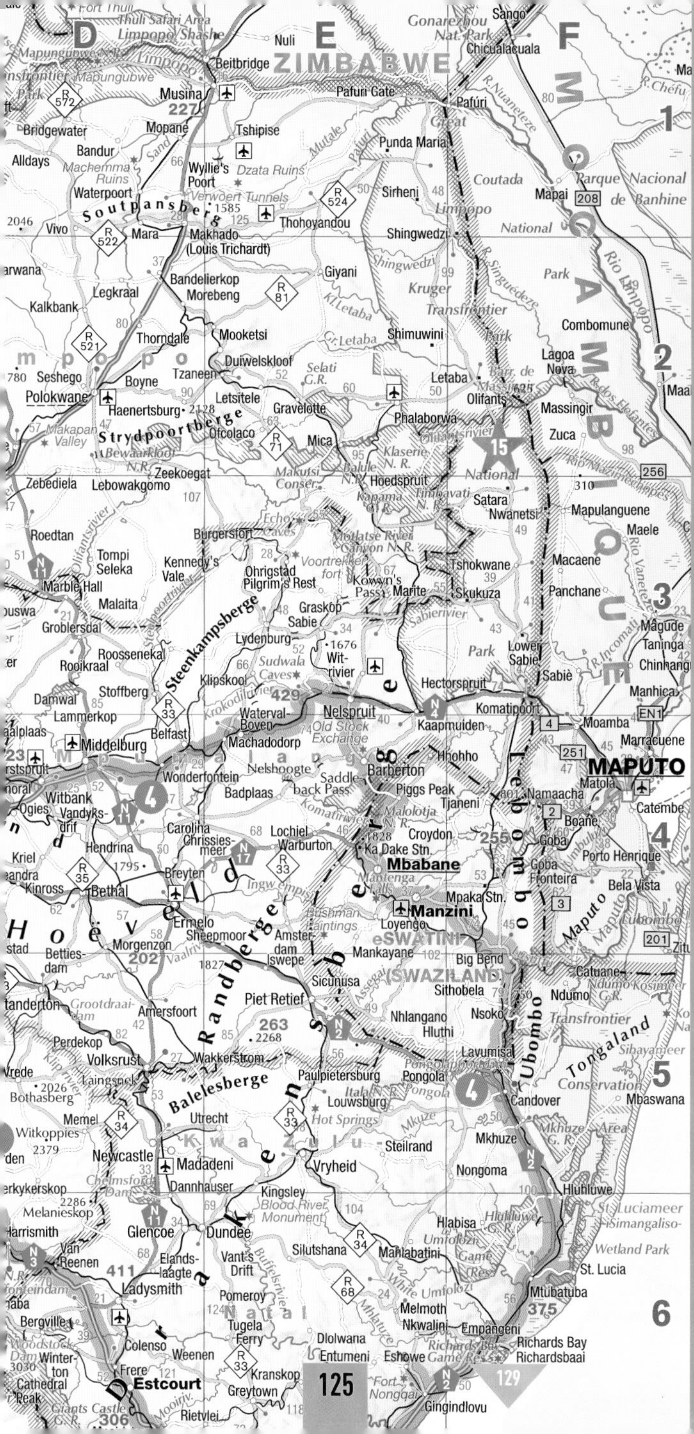
D
E
F
ZIMBABWE
MOÇAMBIQUE
Beitbridge
Musina
Nuli
Mapungubwe N.P.
Limpopo
Mapungubwe Transfrontier Park
Thuli Safari Area
Limpopo/Shashe
Gonarezhou Nat. Park
Sango
Chicualacuala
Pafuri Gate
Pafúri
Bridgewater
Mopane
Tshipise
Punda Maria
Alldays
Bandur
Machemma Ruins
Wyllie's Poort
Dzata Ruins
Waterpoort
Verwoert Tunnels
Sirheni
Coutada
Mapai
Parque Nacional de Banhine
Soutpansberg
Vivo
Mara
Makhado (Louis Trichardt)
Thohoyandou
Shingwedzi
Limpopo National Park
Giyani
Bandelierkop
Morebeng
Legkraal
Kalkbank
Kruger Transfrontier Park
Rio Limpopo
Combomune
Thorndale
Mooketsi
Shimuwini
Duiwelskloof
Letaba
Lagoa Nova
Seshego
Tzaneen
Boyne
Polokwane
Haenertsburg
Letsitele
Gravelotte
Selati G.R.
Olifants
Massingir
Phalaborwa
Zuca
Strydpoortberge
Ofcolaco
Mica
Makapan Valley
Bewaarkloof N.R.
Klaserie N.R.
Balule N.R.
Hoedspruit
Zeekoegat
Zebediela
Lebowakgomo
Makutsi Conser.
Kapama G.R.
Timbavati N.R.
Satara
Nwanetsi
Mapulanguene
Roedtan
Burgersfort
Echo Caves
Motlatse River Canyon N.R.
Maele
Tompi Seleka
Kennedy's Vale
Ohrigstad
Pilgrim's Rest
Voortrekker fort
Kowyn's Pass
Marite
Tshokwane
Macaene
Marble Hall
Malaita
Graskop
Sabie
Skukuza
Panchane
Groblersdal
Steenkampsberge
Lydenburg
Mâgude
Taninga
Roossenekal
Rooikraal
Sudwala Caves
Wit-rivier
Park
Lower Sabie
Chinhanguanine
Sabiè
Stoffberg
Klipskool
Hectorspruit
Manhiça
Damwal
Lammerkop
Waterval-Boven
Nelspruit
Kaapmuiden
Komatipoort
Moamba
Belfast
Old Stock Exchange
Marracuene
Middelburg
Machadodorp
Hhohho
MAPUTO
Mpumalanga
Nelshoogte
Barberton
Matola
Wonderfontein
Saddle-back Pass
Piggs Peak
Namaacha
Catembe
Witbank
Badplaas
Tjaneni
Boane
Ogies
Vandyksdrif
Malolotja N.R.
Lebombo
Carolina
Lochiel
Croydon
Goba
Chrissiesmeer
Warburton
Ka Dake Stn.
Porto Henrique
Kriel
Hendrina
Mbabane
Goba Fronteira
Kinross
Bethal
Breyten
Mantenga Falls
Bela Vista
Mpaka Stn.
Manzini
Bushman Paintings
Loyengo
Hoëveld
Ermelo
Sheepmoor
Amsterdam
eSWATINI (SWAZILAND)
Maputo
Betties-dam
Morgenzon
Iswepe
Mankayane
Big Bend
Catuane
Sicunusa
Sithobela
Ndumo G.R.
Kosimeer
Standerton
Grootdraai-dam
Amersfoort
Piet Retief
Nsoko
Randberge
Nhlangano
Hluthi
Transfrontier
Perdekop
Volksrust
Wakkerstrom
Lavumisa
Tongaland
Sibayameer
Vrede
Laingsnek
Paulpietersburg
Pongola
Pongolapoortdam
Ubombo
Conservation
Bothasberg
Balelesberge
Italal N.R.
Louwsburg
Candover
Mbaswana
Memel
Utrecht
Hot Springs
Mkhuze
Witkoppies
Mkhuze G.R.
Area
KwaZulu-Natal
Steilrand
Newcastle
Madadeni
Vryheid
Nongoma
Chelmsford Dam
Dannhauser
Kingsley
Hluhluwe
Blood River Monument
St. Luciameer
iSimangaliso Wetland Park
Melanieskop
Hlabisa
Hluhluwe G.R.
Harrismith
Glencoe
Dundee
Umfolozi Game Res.
Drakensberg
Van Reenen
Elandslaagte
Vant's Drift
Silutshana
Mahlabatini
St. Lucia
Ladysmith
Buffelsrivier
White Umfolozi
Mtubatuba
Pomeroy
Bergville
Tugela Ferry
Melmoth
Nkwalini
Empangeni
Woodstock Dam
Colenso
Weenen
Dlolwana
Entumeni
Eshowe
Richards Bay Game Res.
Richards Bay
Richardsbaai
Winterton
Frere
Cathedral Peak
Estcourt
Kranskop
Greytown
Fort Nongqai
Gingindlovu
Giants Castle G.R.
Rietvlei
Mooirivier
1
2
3
4
5
6
129

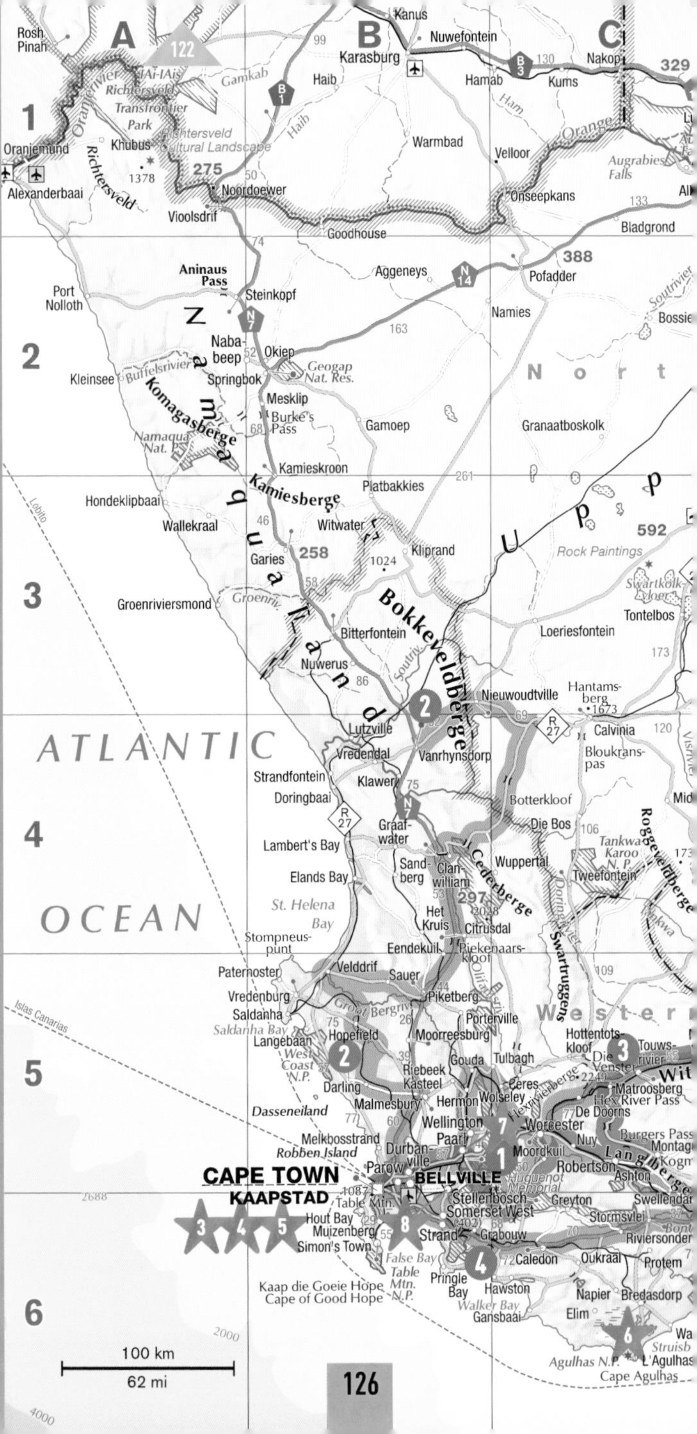
A
B
C
122
1
2
3
4
5
6
Rosh Pinah
Kanus
Nuwefontein
Karasburg
99
Nakop
329
130
Haib
Hamab
Kums
Gamkab
/Ai-/Ais/
Richtersveld
Transfrontier
Park
Oranjerivier
Ham
Orange
Warmbad
Velloor
Augrabies Falls
Oranjemund
Khubus
Richtersveld
Cultural Landscape
Richtersveld
1378
275
50
Noordoewer
Onseepkans
Alexanderbaai
Vioolsdrif
Goodhouse
133
Bladgrond
74
388
Aninaus Pass
Aggeneys
Pofadder
Port Nolloth
Steinkopf
Soutrivier
Namies
Bossie
Nababeep
52
Okiep
163
Geogap Nat. Res.
Kleinsee
Buffelsrivier
Springbok
Namaqualand
Nort
Komagasberge
Mesklip
Burke's Pass
68
Gamoep
Granaatboskolk
Namaqua Nat. P.
Kamieskroon
261
Platbakkies
Hondeklipbaai
Kamiesberge
Upp
Lobito
Wallekraal
46
Witwater
Kliprand
592
Garies
258
1024
Rock Paintings
Swartkolkvloer
58
Groenriviersmond
Groenriv.
Bokkeveldberge
Tontelbos
Bitterfontein
Loeriesfontein
173
Nuwerus
Soutriv.
86
Nieuwoudtville
Hantamsberg
1673
2
Lutzville
69
R 27
Calvinia
120
ATLANTIC
Vredendal
Vanrhynsdorp
Bloukranspas
Strandfontein
Klawer
75
Doringbaai
Botterkloof
N7
R 27
Die Bos
106
Graafwater
Lambert's Bay
Tankwa Karoo N.P.
Roggeveldberge
Sandberg
Clanwilliam
Cederberge
Wuppertal
Tweefontein
Elands Bay
297
St. Helena Bay
53
2028
OCEAN
Het Kruis
Citrusdal
Doringrivier
Tankwa
Stompneuspunt
Eendekuil
Piekenaarskloof
Swartruggens
Paternoster
Velddrif
Sauer
109
Vredenburg
Piketberg
Saldanha
Groot Bergriv.
Porterville
Wester
Islas Canarias
Saldanha Bay
75
26
Langebaan
Hopefield
Moorreesburg
Hottentotskloof
Touwsrivier
West Coast N.P.
2
39
Gouda
Tulbagh
3
Die Venster
Riebeek Kasteel
2249
Darling
Ceres
Matroosberg
Malmesbury
Hermon
Wolseley
Hex River Pass
Dasseneiland
77
60
Wellington
Hexrivierberge
De Doorns
Melkbosstrand
Paarl
7
Worcester
Burgers Pass
Robben Island
Durbanville
57
Nuy
Moordkuil
Montagu
Langeberge
1
CAPE TOWN
KAAPSTAD
Parow
BELLVILLE
Robertson
Ashton
2688
1087
Table Mtn.
Huguenot Memorial
Stellenbosch
Greyton
Swellendam
3
4
5
Hout Bay
Somerset West
Stormsvlei
Muizenberg
8
Strand
402
Grabouw
Riviersonder
Simon's Town
55
70
False Bay
4
Caledon
Oukraal
Protem
Table Mtn. N.P.
Pringle Bay
Kaap die Goeie Hope
Cape of Good Hope
Hawston
Napier
Bredasdorp
Walker Bay
Gansbaai
Elim
6
2000
Struisb
100 km
62 mi
Agulhas N.P.
L'Agulhas
Cape Agulhas
4000

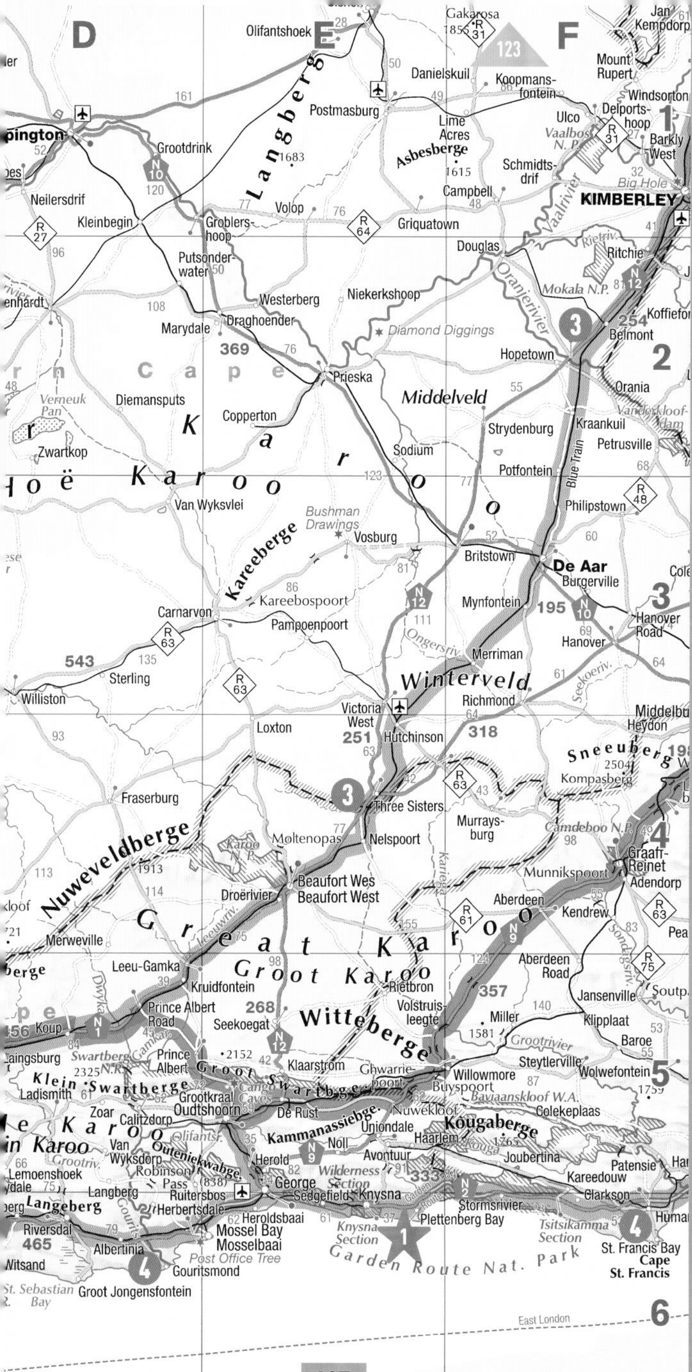
D
E
F
123
1
2
3
4
5
6
Olifantshoek
Gakarosa
Jan Kempdorp
Mount Rupert
Windsorton
Danielskuil
Koopmansfontein
Postmasburg
Langberg
Upington
Grootdrink
Lime Acres
Asbesberge
Ulco
Delportshoop
Barkly West
Vaalbos N.P.
Schmidtsdrif
Campbell
Big Hole
KIMBERLEY
Neilersdrif
Kleinbegin
Groblershoop
Volop
Griquatown
Vaalrivier
Douglas
Riet riv.
Ritchie
Putsonderwater
Mokala N.P.
Oranjerivier
Westerberg
Niekerkshoop
Koffiefontein
Marydale
Draghoender
Diamond Diggings
Belmont
Hopetown
Prieska
Orania
Middelveld
Verneuk Pan
Diemansputs
Copperton
Vanderkloofdam
Kraankuil
Strydenburg
Petrusville
Zwartkop
Sodium
Potfontein
Blue Train
Hoë Karoo
Philipstown
Van Wyksvlei
Bushman Drawings
Kareeberge
Vosburg
Britstown
De Aar
Burgerville
Kareebospoort
Mynfontein
Carnarvon
Hanover Road
Pampoenpoort
Hanover
Ongersriv.
Merriman
Sterling
Williston
Winterveld
Seekoeriv.
Richmond
Victoria West
Middelburg
Loxton
Hutchinson
Heydon
Sneeuberg
Kompasberg
Three Sisters
Fraserburg
Murraysburg
Camdeboo N.P.
Nuweveldberge
Moltenopas
Nelspoort
Karoo N.P.
Graaff-Reinet
Munnikspoort
Adendorp
Beaufort Wes
Beaufort West
Droërivier
Aberdeen
Kendrew
Great Karoo
Merweville
Leeuwriv.
Sondagsriv.
Leeu-Gamka
Groot Karoo
Aberdeen Road
Kruidfontein
Rietbron
Jansenville
Prince Albert Road
Seekoegat
Witteberge
Volstruisleegte
Miller
Klipplaat
Koup
Grootrivier
Baroe
Laingsburg
Swartberg N.R.
Prince Albert
Klaarstrom
Gamka
Steytlerville
Klein Swartberge
Groot Swartberge
Gamkapoort
Willowmore
Wolwefontein
Ladismith
Grootkraal
Cango Caves
Buyspoort
Baviaanskloof W.A.
Zoar
Calitzdorp
Oudtshoorn
De Rust
Nuwekloof
Colekeplaas
Kougaberge
Kammanassiebge.
Uniondale
Haarlem
Olifantsr.
Outeniekwabge.
Noll
Joubertina
Van Wyksdorp
Avontuur
Patensie
Herold
Robinson Pass
Wilderness Section
Kareedouw
Lemoenshoek
Grootriv.
George
Langberg
Ruitersbos
Sedgefield
Knysna
Clarkson
Langeberg
Herbertsdale
Stormsrivier
Heroldsbaai
Plettenberg Bay
Riversdal
Gourits
Mossel Bay
Mosselbaai
Knysna Section
Tsitsikamma Section
Humansdorp
Albertinia
Post Office Tree
St. Francis Bay
Witsand
Gouritsmond
Garden Route Nat. Park
Cape St. Francis
St. Sebastian Bay
Groot Jongensfontein
East London

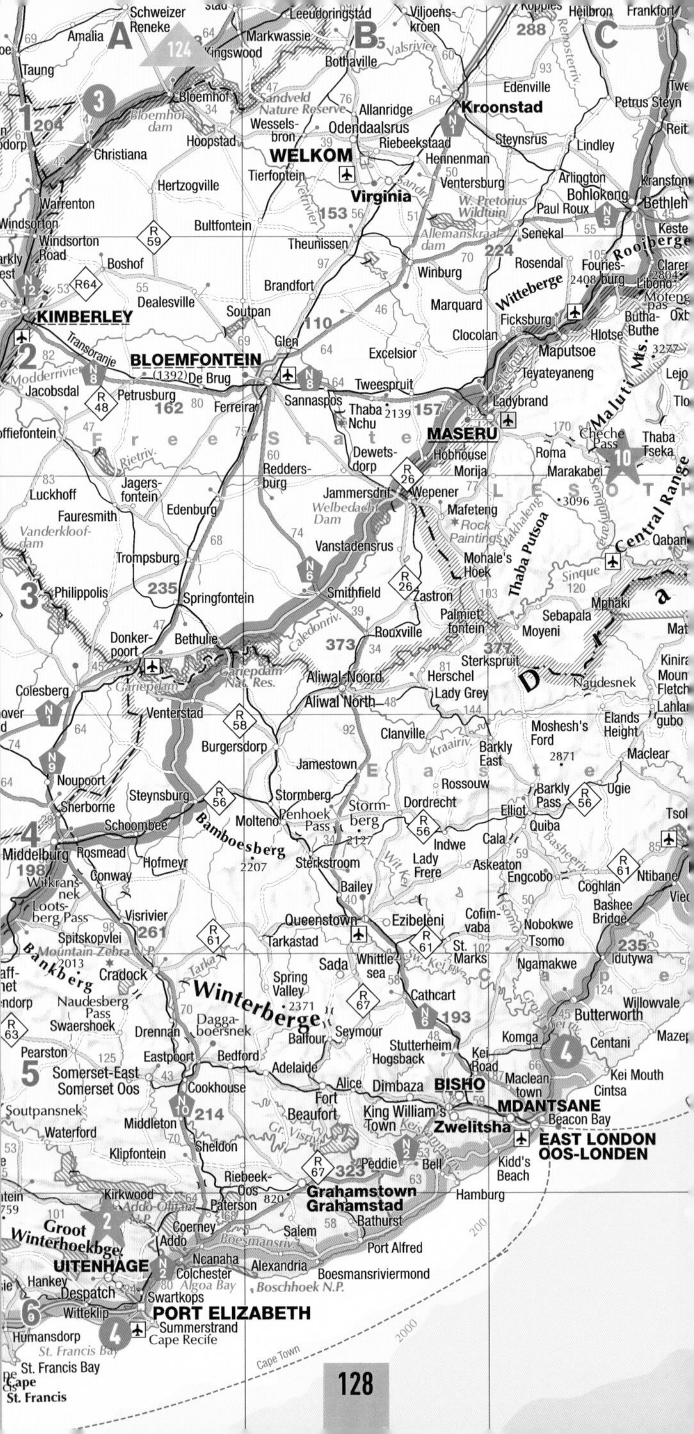
A
B
C
Schweizer Reneke
Amalia
Leeudoringstad
Viljoenskroen
Heilbron
Frankfort
Markwassie
Kingswood
Bothaville
Valsrivier
Taung
Bloemhof
Sandveld Nature Reserve
Allanridge
Kroonstad
Edenville
Petrus Steyn
Bloemhof dam
Wesselsbron
Odendaalsrus
Riebeekstaad
Steynsrus
Lindley
Christiana
Hoopstad
WELKOM
Hennenman
Tierfontein
Ventersburg
Arlington
Bohlokong
Bethlehem
Hertzogville
Virginia
Sand
W. Pretorius Wildtuin
Paul Roux
Warrenton
Windsorton
Windsorton Road
Bultfontein
Allemanskraal dam
Senekal
Theunissen
Rosendal
Rooiberge
Boshof
Winburg
Fouriesburg
Brandfort
Witteberge
Dealesville
Marquard
Soutpan
KIMBERLEY
Ficksburg
Clocolan
Butha-Buthe
Hlotse
Glen
Excelsior
Maputsoe
Transoranje
BLOEMFONTEIN
Teyateyaneng
(1392) De Brug
Tweespruit
Modderrivier
Jacobsdal
Petrusburg
Ferreira
Sannaspos
Thaba Nchu
2139
Ladybrand
Maseru
Maluti Mts.
Koffiefontein
Free State
Rietriv.
Dewetsdorp
Hobhouse
Roma
Cheche Pass
Thaba Tseka
Reddersburg
Morija
Marakabei
Jagersfontein
Jammersdrif
Wepener
LESOTHO
Central Range
Luckhoff
Fauresmith
Edenburg
Welbedacht Dam
Mafeteng
3096
Vanderkloofdam
Rock Paintings
Makhaleng
Thaba Putsoa
Senqunyane
Qaba
Trompsburg
Vanstadensrus
Mohale's Hoek
Sinque
Philippolis
Springfontein
Smithfield
Zastron
Mphaki
Caledonriv.
Palmietfontein
Sebapala
Moyeni
Donkerpoort
Bethulie
Rouxville
Sterkspruit
Gariepdam Nat. Res.
Gariepdam
Aliwal-Noord
Aliwal North
Herschel
Lady Grey
Drakensberg
Naudesnek
Colesberg
Venterstad
Moshesh's Ford
Elands Height
Clanville
Burgersdorp
Kraairiv.
Barkly East
2871
Maclear
Noupoort
Jamestown
Eastern
Rossouw
Ugie
Steynsburg
Stormberg
Barkly Pass
Sherborne
Molteno
Penhoek Pass
Stormberg
Dordrecht
Elliot
Schoombee
Bamboesberg
2127
Indwe
Quiba
Middelburg
Rosmead
Hofmeyr
2207
Sterkstroom
Cala
Lady Frere
Askeaton
Engcobo
Bashee riv.
Coghlan
Ntibane
Witkransnek
Conway
Bailey
Lootsberg Pass
Visrivier
Queenstown
Ezibeleni
Cofimvaba
Nobokwe
Bashee Bridge
Spitskopvlei
Tarkastad
Tsomo
Mountain Zebra N.P.
2013
Cradock
Tarka
Sada
Whittlesea
St. Marks
Ngamakwe
Idutywa
Bankberg
Spring Valley
Winterberge
2371
Cathcart
Cape
Naudesberg Pass
Willowvale
Swaershoek
Dagga-boersnek
Butterworth
Drennan
Balfour
Seymour
Pearston
Stutterheim
Komga
Centani
Eastpoort
Bedford
Hogsback
Kei Road
Kei Mouth
Somerset-East
Somerset Oos
Adelaide
Alice
Dimbaza
BISHO
Maclean-town
Cintsa
Cookhouse
Fort Beaufort
King William's Town
MDANTSANE
Beacon Bay
Soutpansnek
Middleton
Zwelitsha
EAST LONDON
OOS-LONDEN
Waterford
Sheldon
Klipfontein
Peddie
Bell
Kidd's Beach
Riebeek-Oos
Grahamstown
Grahamstad
Hamburg
Kirkwood
Addo-Olifant N.P.
Paterson
Groot Winterhoekbge.
Coerney
Bathurst
Salem
Addo
Boesmansriv.
Port Alfred
UITENHAGE
Ncanaha
Alexandria
Colchester
Boesmansriviermond
Hankey
Algoa Bay
Boschhoek N.P.
Despatch
Swartkops
Witteklip
PORT ELIZABETH
Humansdorp
Summerstrand
Cape Recife
St. Francis Bay
St. Francis Bay
Cape St. Francis
Cape Town

D
E
F
125
1
2
3
4
5
6
Perdekop
Volksrust
Wakkerstroom
Vrede
Bothasberg
Laingsnek
Balelesberge
Paulpietersburg
Louwsburg
Hot Springs
Pongola
Lavumisa
Sibayameer
Lubombo
Mbaswana
Transfrontier
Conservation
Memel
Witkoppies
Utrecht
Newcastle
Madadeni
Kwa Zulu
Vryheid
Steilrand
Mkhuze
Mkhuze G. R.
Nongoma
Hluhluwe
St. Luciameer
iSimangaliso-
Wetland Park
Chelmsford Dam
Dannhauser
Kingsley
Blood River Monument
Melanieskop
Glencoe
Dundee
Harrismith
Van Reenen
Elandslaagte
Vant's Drift
Silutshana
Mahlabatini
Hlabisa
Hluhluwe G. R.
Umfolozi Game Res.
St. Lucia
Mtubatuba
Ladysmith
Pomeroy
Buffelsrivier
White Umfolozi
Melmoth
Empangeni
Richards Bay
Richardsbaai
Richards Bay Game Res.
Bergville
Colenso
Natal
Dlolwana
Nkwalini
Eshowe
Woodstock Dam
Winterton
Weenen
Tugela Ferry
Cathedral Peak
Frere
Estcourt
Kranskop
Entumeni
Fort Nongqai
Gingindlovu
Greytown
Tugela
Giants Castle G. R.
Mooirivier
Rietvlei
Fort Mtobeni
Giants Castle
New Hanover
Fawnleas
Darnall
Nottingham Road
Howick
New Hanover
Stanger
Lower Loteni
PIETERMARITZ-BURG
Shakaskraal
Waterfall
Edendale
Tongaat
Verulam
Mzimkulwana
Underberg
Bulwer
Mpumalanga
Kwa-Mashu
Richmond
Pinetown
DURBAN
Donnybrook
Isipingo
Amanzimtoti
Umbumbulu
Mkomazi
Kingsburg
Ixopo
Umzimkulu
Umzinto
Umkomaas
Franklin
Highflats
Park Rynie
Sezela
Harding
Oribi Gorge
Hibberdene
Sea Park
Port Shepstone
Bizana
Mount Ayliff
Magusheni
Ramsgate
Flagstaff
Port Edward
Mkambati N. R.
Umtentu
Lusikisiki
Port Grosvenor
Port St. Johns
Beira
Manakara
INDIAN
OCEAN
100 km
62 mi

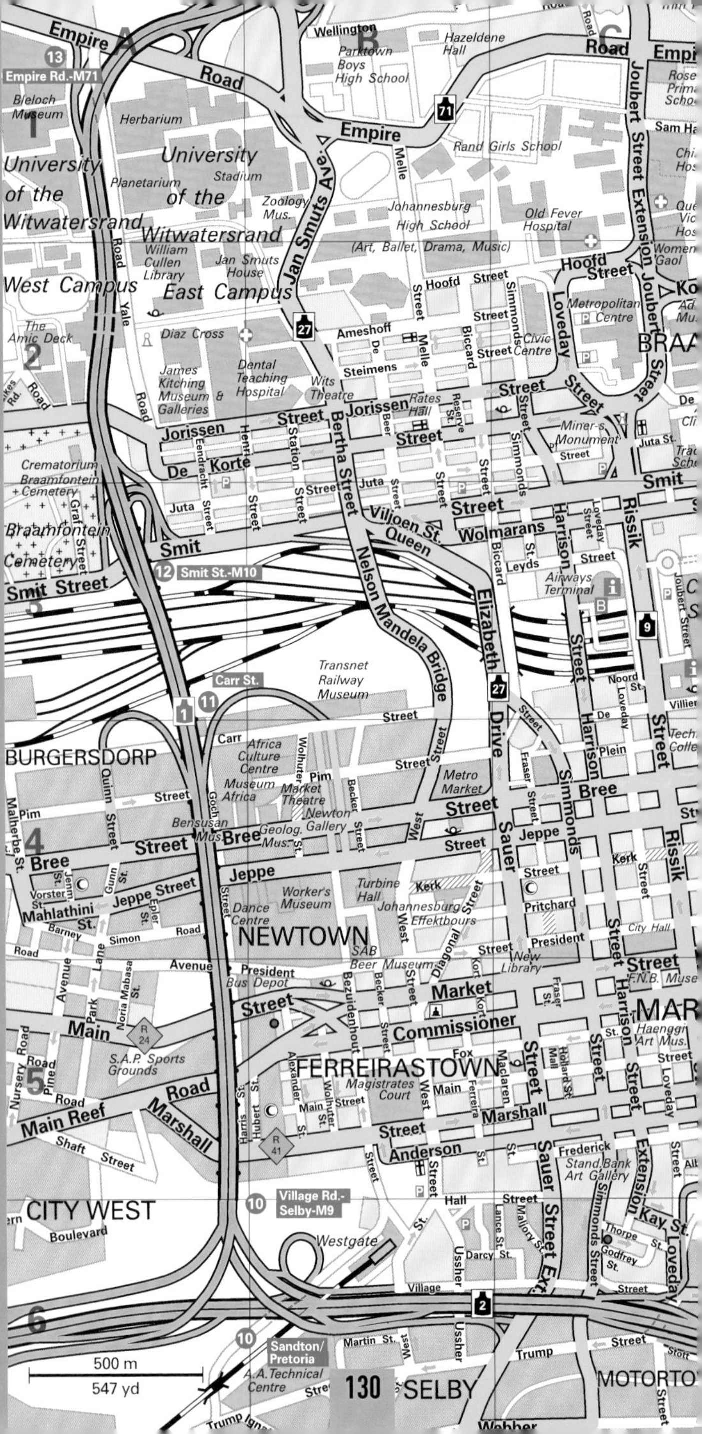

A
B
C
1
2
3
4
5
6
Empire Road
Empire Rd.-M71
13
Wellington
Parktown Boys High School
Hazeldene Hall
Road
Joubert Street Extension
Rosebank Primary School
Sam Hancock
Bleloch Museum
Herbarium
University of the Witwatersrand
Planetarium
Stadium
Zoology Mus.
Jan Smuts Ave.
Empire
Melle
Rand Girls School
71
Johannesburg High School
(Art, Ballet, Drama, Music)
Old Fever Hospital
Women's Gaol
William Cullen Library
Jan Smuts House
West Campus
East Campus
Yale Road
Hoofd Street
Simmonds
Loveday
Metropolitan Centre
Civic Centre
Braamfontein
The Amic Deck
Diaz Cross
27
Ameshoff
De Beer
Biccard
Steimens
James Kitching Museum & Galleries
Dental Teaching Hospital
Wits Theatre
Rates Hall
Reserve St.
Jorissen Street
Miner's Monument
Juta St.
Crematorium Braamfontein Cemetery
Braamfontein Cemetery
Eendracht
Henri Street
Station Street
Bertha Street
De Korte Street
Juta Street
Smit Street
Graf Street
Viljoen St.
Queen
Wolmarans
Harrison Street
Rissik Street
Leyds St.
Airways Terminal
Smit St.-M10
12
Nelson Mandela Bridge
Elizabeth
Transnet Railway Museum
9
Carr St.
11
1
Noord St.
De Villiers
Plein
Technical College
BURGERSDORP
Carr Street
Africa Culture Centre
Wolhuter
Pim
Museum Africa
Market Theatre
Newton Gallery
Becker
Metro Market
Sauer Drive
Fraser Street
Bree Street
Quinn Street
Malherbe St.
Goch
Bensusan Mus.
Geolog. Mus.
West Street
Jeppe Street
Kerk Street
Pritchard
Jenner St.
Gunn St.
Vorster St.
Mahlathini St.
Epler St.
Jeppe Street
Dance Centre
Worker's Museum
Turbine Hall
Johannesburg Effektbours
Diagonal Street
City Hall
Barney Road
Simon
NEWTOWN
SAB Beer Museum
President Street
New Library
F.N.B. Museum
Avenue
Park Lane
Noria Mabasa St.
Bus Depot
Bezuidenhout
Market Street
Kort
Fraser St.
MARSHALLTOWN
Main
R 24
Commissioner
Haenggi Art Mus.
Nursery Road
Pine Road
S.A.P. Sports Grounds
FERREIRASTOWN
Alexander
Magistrates Court
Fox
Maclaren
Ferreira
Mall
Hollard St.
Main Reef Road
Marshall
Harris St.
Hubert St.
R 41
Anderson
Frederick
Stand.Bank Art Gallery
Shaft Street
Hall Street
Sauer Street Ext.
Kay St.
Thorpe St.
Godfrey St.
CITY WEST
Boulevard
Village Rd.-Selby-M9
10
Westgate
Lance St.
Mallory St.
Darcy St.
Ussher
Village
2
Martin St.
Trump Street
Sandton/Pretoria
A.A. Technical Centre
500 m
547 yd
SELBY
MOTORTOWN
Webber

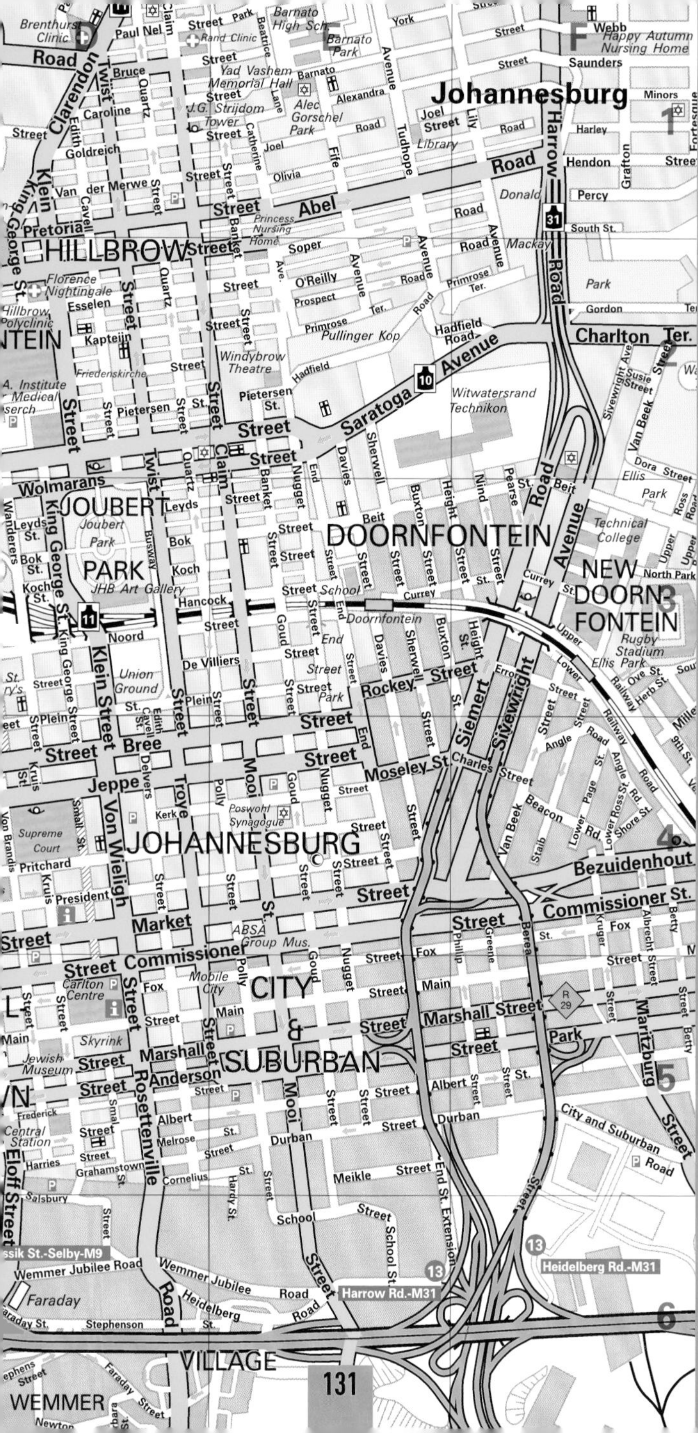
Brenthurst Clinic
Rand Clinic
Barnato High Sch.
Barnato Park
Webb
Happy Autumn Nursing Home
Saunders
Johannesburg
Minors
Yad Vashem Memorial Hall
J.G. Strijdom Tower
Alec Gorschel Park
Alexandra
Joel Street
Library
Harley
Hendon
Grafton
Percy
Clarendon
Twist
Bruce
Quartz
Caroline
Edith
Goldreich
Van der Merwe
Cavell
Klein
King George St.
Pretoria
Abel
Princess Nursing Home
Donald
South St.
HILLBROW
Soper
O'Reilly
Prospect
Mackay
Primrose Ter.
Park
Gordon
Florence Nightingale
Hillbrow Polyclinic
Esselen
Kapteijn
Friedenskirche
Pullinger Kop
Hadfield Road
Charlton Ter.
Windybrow Theatre
Pietersen St.
Saratoga Avenue
Witwatersrand Technikon
Sivewright Ave
Susie Street
Van Beek
A. Institute Medical Research
Pietersen
Wolmarans
Leyds
Banket
Nugget
Davies
Shervell
Buxton
Height
Nind
Pearse
Beit
Dora Street
Ellis Park
Ross
Technical College
JOUBERT PARK
Joubert Park
JHB Art Gallery
Busway
Bok
Koch
Hancock
DOORNFONTEIN
Currey
NEW DOORNFONTEIN
North Park
Upper
Rugby Stadium
Ellis Park
Doornfontein
School
End
Goud
Noord
Wanderers
Union Ground
De Villiers
Plein
Rockey Street
Siemert
Sivewright
Errol
Lower
Railway
Ove St.
Herb St.
Angle
Page St.
Bree
Delvers
Troye
Mooi
Polly
Moseley St.
Charles Street
Beacon
Staib
Jeppe
Kerk
Poswohl Synagogue
Supreme Court
Small St.
Von Wielligh
JOHANNESBURG
Pritchard
Kruis
President
Market
Bezuidenhout
Commissioner St.
ABSA Group Mus.
Fox
Philip
Greene
Berea
Kruger
Albrecht
Betty
Carlton Centre
Mobile City
CITY & SUBURBAN
Main
Marshall Street
R 29
Maritzburg
Skyrink
Jewish Museum
Anderson
Rissik
Albert
Frederick
Central Station
Eloff Street
Harries
Melrose
Grahamstown
Cornelius
Hardy St.
Rosettenville
Durban
City and Suburban Road
Meikle
End St. Extension
Salsbury
School Street
Ossik St.-Selby-M9
Heidelberg Rd.-M31
Wemmer Jubilee Road
Harrow Rd.-M31
Faraday
Heidelberg Road
Stephenson St.
VILLAGE
WEMMER
Faraday Street
Harrow Road
Van Brandis
Streets
10
11
13
31
1
2
3
4
5
6
D
E
F

KEY TO ROAD ATLAS

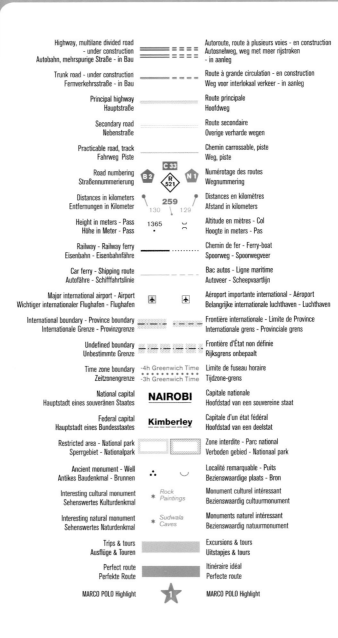

Highway, multilane divided road - under construction Autobahn, mehrspurige Straße - in Bau		Autoroute, route à plusieurs voies - en construction Autosnelweg, weg met meer rijstroken - in aanleg
Trunk road - under construction Fernverkehrsstraße - in Bau		Route à grande circulation - en construction Weg voor interlokaal verkeer - in aanleg
Principal highway Hauptstraße		Route principale Hoofdweg
Secondary road Nebenstraße		Route secondaire Overige verharde wegen
Practicable road, track Fahrweg Piste		Chemin carrossable, piste Weg, piste
Road numbering Straßennummerierung	B 2 C 33 R 521 N 1	Numérotage des routes Wegnummering
Distances in kilometers Entfernungen in Kilometer	259 130 129	Distances en kilomètres Afstand in kilometers
Height in meters - Pass Höhe in Meter - Pass	1365	Altitude en mètres - Col Hoogte in meters - Pas
Railway - Railway ferry Eisenbahn - Eisenbahnfähre		Chemin de fer - Ferry-boat Spoorweg - Spoorwegveer
Car ferry - Shipping route Autofähre - Schifffahrtslinie		Bac autos - Ligne maritime Autoveer - Scheepvaartlijn
Major international airport - Airport Wichtiger internationaler Flughafen - Flughafen		Aéroport importante international - Aéroport Belangrijke internationale luchthaven - Luchthaven
International boundary - Province boundary Internationale Grenze - Provinzgrenze		Frontière internationale - Limite de Province Internationale grens - Provinciale grens
Undefined boundary Unbestimmte Grenze		Frontière d'État non définie Rijksgrens onbepaalt
Time zone boundary Zeitzonengrenze	-4h Greenwich Time -3h Greenwich Time	Limite de fuseau horaire Tijdzone-grens
National capital Hauptstadt eines souveränen Staates	NAIROBI	Capitale nationale Hoofdstad van een souvereine staat
Federal capital Hauptstadt eines Bundesstaates	Kimberley	Capitale d'un état fédéral Hoofdstad van een deelstat
Restricted area - National park Sperrgebiet - Nationalpark		Zone interdite - Parc national Verboden gebied - Nationaal park
Ancient monument - Well Antikes Baudenkmal - Brunnen		Localité remarquable - Puits Bezienswaardige plaats - Bron
Interesting cultural monument Sehenswertes Kulturdenkmal	Rock Paintings	Monument culturel intéressant Bezienswaardig cultuurmonument
Interesting natural monument Sehenswertes Naturdenkmal	Sudwala Caves	Monuments naturel intéressant Bezienswaardig natuurmonument
Trips & tours Ausflüge & Touren		Excursions & tours Uitstapjes & tours
Perfect route Perfekte Route		Itinéraire idéal Perfecte route
MARCO POLO Highlight	1	MARCO POLO Highlight

INDEX

This index lists all places and sights, plus the names of important people and key words featured in this guide. Numbers in bold indicate a main entry.

WRITE TO US

e-mail: info@marcopologuides.co.uk

Did you have a great holiday?
Is there something on your mind?
Whatever it is, let us know!
Whether you want to praise, alert us to errors or give us a personal tip – MARCO POLO would be pleased to hear from you.
We do everything we can to provide the very latest information for your trip.
Nevertheless, despite all of our authors' thorough research, errors can creep in. MARCO POLO does not accept any liability for this. Please contact us by e-mail or post.

MARCO POLO Travel Publishing Ltd
Pinewood, Chineham Business Park
Crockford Lane, Chineham
Basingstoke, Hampshire RG24 8AL
United Kingdom

PICTURE CREDITS

Cover photograph: Giraffes (mauritius images: S. Bloom)
Abseil Africa (17 top); Norman Catherine (16 centre); Simon Deiner/SDR Photo (16 top); W. Dieterich (12/13, 28, 29, 36, 43, 50, 60, 65, 100/101); DuMont Bildarchiv (23); DuMont Bildarchiv: Kiedrowski/Schwarz (20, 34, 89), Selbach (2 centre bottom, 32/33, 59, 82, 110 top); J. Frangenberg (5); W. Gartung (28/29, 30 left, 39, 40, 68, 76, 94/95, 97); Getty Images/Gallo Images: de la Harpe (1 top); Huber: Bäck (124/125), Damm (3 top, 66/67, 79), Huber (front flap right, 2 bottom, 3 centre, 48/49, 56, 72/73, 86/87), Orient (57, 63), Picture Finders (78), Ripani (52), Giovanni Simeone (10/11, 18/19, 108/109, 133); © iStockphoto.com: Petoo (16 bottom); A. Kreß-Zorn (113); Laif: Emmler (15, 42, 45, 70, 74, 90, 96, 107, 108, 109), Huber (117); Laif/ Le Figaro Magazine: Fautre (77); mauritius images: AGE (46), Alamy (2 top, 2 centretop, 4, 6, 7, 8, 9, 24/25, 26 right, 27, 30 right, 54, 84, 93, 98/99, 102, 110 bottom), Food and Drink (26 left); World Pictures (front flap left); centre Mauthe (3 bottom, 80/81); H. Mielke (38, 111); ON BROADWAY: Gerhard Enslin (17 bottom); D. Schumacher (1 bottom); White Star: Friedrichsmeier (104/105)

1st Edition 2012
Worldwide Distribution: Marco Polo Travel Publishing Ltd, Pinewood, Chineham Business Park, Crockford Lane, Basingstoke, Hampshire RG24 8AL, United Kingdom. Email: sales@marcopolouk.com

Chief editors: Michaela Lienemann (concept, managing editor), Marion Zorn (concept, text editor)
Author: Dagmar Schumacher; editor: Manfred Pötzscher
Programme supervision: Anita Dahlinger, Ann-Katrin Kutzner, Nikolai Michaelis
Picture editor: Gabriele Forst
What's hot: wunder media, Munich
Cartography road atlas & pull-out map: © MAIRDUMONT, Ostfildern
Design: milchhof : atelier, Berlin; Front cover, pull-out map cover, page 1: factor product munich
Translated from German by Birgitt Lederer; editor of the English edition: Margaret Howie, fullproof.co.za
Prepress: M. Feuerstein, Wigel

Printed in Germany on non-chlorine bleached paper

DOS & DON'TS

A few things you should bear in mind in South Africa

DO BE ON THE LOOKOUT FOR PEOPLE CROSSING THE MOTORWAY

Overseas tourists may find it inconceivable that pedestrians and animals will cross the motorway. In South Africa it is quite commonplace so drivers should be cautious and aware. It is also not an uncommon sight to see horses, cattle and sheep grazing on the grass verges of motorways.

DO NOT ROLL DOWN YOUR CAR WINDOW

Beggars are a common sight at many traffic lights. Do not open your car window to give them money. By supporting them you will only exacerbate the problem. Your good intentions may also backfire as their lightning speed fingers grab whatever they can lay their hands on – handbags, wallets, jewellery and expensive sunglasses.

DO NOT FEED THE ANIMALS

As a rule the feeding of animals is prohibited in all game parks. Even the baboons that roam freely alongside roads and near rest spots should not be fed. Sadly they have completely lost their fear of man and when a car stops they will not hesitate to climb on the roof. If you dare open a car door they will be inside in no time scrounging for food and will eat everything and anything edible or not that they can lay their hands on. Many a woman's handbag – with passport, papers and all – has fallen into the hands of these primate thieves.

DO BE WARY OF GIVING SOMEONE A RIDE

With public transport being erratic in some areas it is not an uncommon sight to see people hitchhiking. They will be picked up by other willing locals in no time. Tourists on the other hand should exercise caution and avoid picking up hitchhikers. It will be impossible for you to gauge whether it is safe to give someone a ride.

DO NOT TRUST ZEBRA CROSSINGS

As disciplined as South Africans are when it comes to queuing up, discipline goes right out the door when it comes to how they behave in traffic. The cardinal rule is that as a pedestrian – particularly in Cape Town – you cannot go by the assumption that the driver of a vehicle will stop for you just because you are about to cross a street at a zebra crossing. On the other hand, if you are behind the wheel, never go by the assumption that pedestrians will stop at a red traffic light – the saving grace is that you can be sure that cars will stop at a red light!